A Fair Sort
of
Battering

Also in this series:

A Fair Sort
of
Battering

EDITED BY MEGAN HUTCHING

HarperCollins*Publishers*

in association with the Ministry for Culture and Heritage

National Library of New Zealand Cataloguing-in-Publication Data
A fair sort of battering : New Zealanders remember the Italian
campaign / edited by Megan Hutching.
Previous ed.: 2004.
Includes index.
ISBN 978-1-86950-785-5
1. New Zealand. Army—Biography. 2. World War, 1939-1945—
Personal narratives, New Zealand. 3. World War, 1939-1945—
Campaigns—Italy. 4. Soldiers—New Zealand—Biography.
I. Hutching, Megan.
940.54215—dc 22

First published 2009
HarperCollins*Publishers (New Zealand) Limited*

P.O. Box 1, Shortland Street, Auckland

ISBN 978 1 86950 785 5

Cover design by Louise McGeachie
Front cover images: (top) detail of Soldiers at Cassino, Italy, photographer
George Frederick Kaye, 1914–2004, DA-005454, War History Collection,
Alexander Turnbull Library, Wellington, New Zealand; (bottom) Monastery
ruins at Montecassino, photographer L.H. Ross, fl 1939–1945, DA-03751, War
History Collection, Alexander Turnbull Library, Wellington, New Zealand
Back cover image: Soldiers at Cassino, Italy, photographer George
Frederick Kaye, 1914–2004, DA-005454, War History Collection,
Alexander Turnbull Library, Wellington, New Zealand
Internal design and typesetting by Springfield West
Printed by Griffin Press, Australia

70gsm Classic used by HarperCollins*Publishers* is a natural,
recyclable product made from wood grown in sustainable
forests. The manufacturing processes conform to the
environmental regulations in the country of origin, Finland.

This book is dedicated to my uncle,
Private F.E. (Eddie) Leabourn,
and all those like him who fought against fascism
in Italy during the Second World War.

M.H.

CONTENTS

PREFACE

Elizabeth Bowen, the novelist, wrote that '[t]he charm, one might say the genius of memory, is that it is choosy, chancy and temperamental; it rejects the edifying cathedral and indelibly photographs the small boy outside, chewing a hunk of melon in the dust.' Through the filter of 60-odd years, you are about to read thirteen people's experiences of both the 'small boys' — the day to day life of war — and the 'cathedrals' — the danger, excitement and chaos of being in action. The book does this for a reason: war is not only fighting. Much of it is to do with getting on with other people, training, meeting civilians, coming to terms with loss, sightseeing, dealing with the chores of everyday life — washing, eating, drinking. I hope that when you have read this book, you will have some idea of what it was like to go to war.

In Italy during the Second World War, the New Zealand forces came into close contact with civilians — in many instances they lived in their houses — and had to fight their way the length of a country which was full of built history, but also of mountains and river valleys where all the seasons were experienced vividly. Most who fought in, around or above Italy came away with a lifelong attachment to the place.

Here we have the stories of thirteen men and women who participated in the Allied campaign in Italy. Not all fought on the ground — there is a sailor in the Royal Navy, and a pilot in the Fleet Air Arm. The experiences recounted here also remind us that not every person who goes to war is involved in front-line action. We have a nurse who nursed at 2 New Zealand General Hospital in Caserta, a Tui who worked in the

New Zealand Forces Clubs in Bari and Rome, a dentist, and a padre, as well as those at the sharpest point of the 'sharp end' — infantrymen, some 'tankies' and a sapper.

Roberto Rabel has written the introductory essay. He provides a context for the interviews with an outline of the strategy and progress of the campaign. He has also used individuals' experiences to write more generally about some of the themes and arguments regarding New Zealand and the role of New Zealanders in the Second World War.

In this book I have used six interviews that I did not record myself — it therefore reflects the different approaches of each interviewer. I am extremely grateful to Roberto Rabel for allowing me to use the interviews with Rae Familton, Gordon Slatter, Jack Somerville and Isobelle Wright, which he commissioned Aaron Fox to record in the late 1990s. I am equally grateful to Liz Catherall, who allowed me to use the interviews which she recorded with Reg Hermans and with her mother, Pat Hamilton. My grateful thanks also go to Isobelle Wright, Rae Familton and Reg Hermans for allowing me to use their interviews, and to Marie Slatter and the Somerville family for giving me permission to include the interviews with Gordon Slatter and Jack Somerville.

My colleagues in the History Group, Ian McGibbon, Neill Atkinson and Bronwyn Dalley, gave, as always, extremely useful feedback on the drafts of the stories that you are about to read. David Green has edited them with his usual care and tact. Alison Parr, who has recently begun to work with me on this project, found most of the wonderful photographs in the book. I cannot express how grateful I am for her assistance as I hurtled towards a very tight deadline. She is a delight to work with and has augmented my enthusiasm for this project.

In order to find people for the interviews that I recorded, I began by publicising the project and asking men who had fought in the Italian campaign to contact me. I sent respondents a lengthy questionnaire asking them about their experiences.

All the questionnaires and other accounts that I have received will eventually be deposited with Archives New Zealand in Wellington so that they will be available to researchers in the future. My recordings of the interviews and accompanying material will be archived at the Oral History Centre at the Alexander Turnbull Library in Wellington, where they will be available to researchers subject to any conditions placed on them by the interviewees. The words that appear in this book are just a small proportion of those recorded in the interviews. While I have tried to preserve the informal language of the interviews — because I wanted to keep them close to the way in which people spoke — each has been heavily edited.

I am also grateful to those who filled in my questionnaire, either themselves or on behalf of someone else. I have been fortunate to receive accounts from people of their or their relative's experiences during the war, which I very much appreciated. Others sent photographs.

I was the recipient of wonderful hospitality as I travelled around recording these interviews. It was a pleasure to find that home baking is not a thing of the past. Others I must thank include the Prime Minister, Helen Clark, for her continuing interest in this series of books; the Royal New Zealand

Returned Services Association and Age Concern, who helped to publicise this project; Gwen Calnon, who made my travel so uncomplicated and helped with ordering the photographs; Aaron Fox; Linda Evans and the staff at the Alexander Turnbull Library's Oral History Centre; John Sullivan and the staff at the Turnbull's photographic archive; Joan McCracken and her colleagues from Turnbull Library Pictures; Olwen Morgan at the Navy Museum in Auckland; Monty Soutar, Sonny Sewell and Charlie Bell for their help in finding 28 (Maori) Battalion veterans; Ross Somerville; the Australian War Memorial; and the team at HarperCollins, especially Sue Page for her usual enthusiasm, tact and consideration during the production of this book.

As always, I have had the support of my friends and family, all of whom are constantly surprised by my esoteric (and uncharacteristic) knowledge of things military, and all of whom are kind enough still to display interest when I say those dreaded words, 'Listen to this . . .' Thanks to you all.

Megan Hutching
August 2003

GLOSSARY

2-i-c	second in command
2NZEF	Second New Zealand Expeditionary Force
ack ack	anti-aircraft
ADS	Advanced Dressing Station
AMGOT	Allied Military Government of Occupied Territory
ASDIC	Allied Submarine Detection Investigation Committee, sonar
bivvy	bivouac
Bren	British light machine gun
brewed up	a vehicle in flames after being fired upon
casa	house
CCS	Casualty Clearing Station
civvy	civilian
demob	demobilisation
Div	Division(al), usually 2nd New Zealand Division
Don R	despatch rider
DSM	Distinguished Service Medal
Ech	Echelon
ENSA	Entertainments National Service Association, British equivalent of Kiwi Concert Party
flag lieutenant	aide to the commanding officer (Navy)
GH	General Hospital
Gib	Gibraltar
Ities	Italians
Jerry	Germans
jimmy-the-one	first lieutenant
LC	landing craft
LCS	landing craft, support
LCT	landing craft, tank
MC	Military Cross
MDS	Main Dressing Station
Me-109	Messerschmitt 109, German fighter plane

MID	Mentioned in Despatches
MM	Military Medal
MO	medical officer
mortar	a short-range, high-angle artillery weapon
MP	military policeman
NAAFI	Navy Army Air Force Institute, canteen
NZEF	New Zealand Expeditionary Force
O Pip	observation post
OR	other rank(s)
para	paratrooper
POW	prisoner of war
RAP	Regimental Aid Post
Red Cap	military policeman
RNVR	Royal Naval Volunteer Reserve
RSM	Regimental Sergeant Major
S-mine	cylindrical-shaped metal canister, with a spring mechanism, filled with shrapnel
sapper	military engineer
SAS	Special Air Service
sig	signaller or signalman
Spandau	German machine gun
stonk	type of concentrated artillery bombardment
suffragi	Egyptian waiter
Ted(s)	*Tedeschi*, Italian word for Germans
Teller mine	German anti-tank mine
Tommy	English soldier
Tommy gun	sub-machine gun
two-pipper	lieutenant
VAD	Voluntary Aid Detachment nurse
White scout car	American-made open-topped scout car
WRNS	Women's Royal Naval Service, often called Wrens
WWSA	Women's War Service Auxiliary
Yanks	Americans

INTRODUCTION

Up the strada: remembering the Italian campaign

Roberto Rabel

AGE HAD NOT WEARIED THEM. As octogenarians, Gordon and Luciana Johnston exhibited a mutual zest for life undiminished by the many years that had passed since the fortunes of war first threw them together in May 1945 in Trieste, a battle-scarred city at the northern end of the Adriatic. Over Sunday afternoon coffee, we chatted about their still vivid recollections of the day at the end of the war when Gordon decided to pose as a local Triestine and nonchalantly strolled past the sentries positioned at the entry to a private bathing enclosure which was technically off limits to New Zealand soldiers. It was a fateful decision. His chance meeting there with Luciana transformed both their lives forever. For Gordon and Luciana Johnston, New Zealand participation in the Italian campaign of the Second World War had the happiest of outcomes.

Gordon Johnston was one of tens of thousands of New Zealanders who fought their way up the boot of Italy from 1943 to 1945 as part of the vast multinational force assembled to roll back Axis aggression in far-flung theatres of war across the globe. Constituting a significant cohort of their nation's manhood, almost all the New Zealanders who served in Italy did so as members of a nationally distinctive unit, which they knew affectionately as the 'Div' — the 2nd New Zealand Division. Although they were despatched to Italy for the grim purpose of conducting war, the New Zealanders who served in the Div also shared in a collective experience comparable in social and cultural terms to that of participating in an oversized, prolonged rugby tour of a single nation. 'It was a slice of New Zealand transplanted overseas,' as one veteran of the campaign observes in this book. The experience of these soldiers in Italy reinforced their sense of themselves as New Zealanders, and their faith in the essential decency of their fellow Kiwis. If predominantly a male affair, it was not exclusively so, for the New Zealand forces in Italy included a small number of intrepid women who served mainly as nurses or 'Tuis' — members of the Women's War Service Auxiliary. Together, these men and women ensured that there was a singularly New Zealand contribution to the defeat of Hitler's armies in one particular theatre of war.

Their collective achievement is especially worthy of remembrance and commemoration in 2009, which marks the 65th anniversary of one of the most hard-fought battles in Italy — the battle for Cassino. This book brings together a series of interviews with a representative range of the New Zealand men and women responsible for that achievement. The stories recounted in these interviews are important because they remind us that, while wars are resolved collectively, they are lived individually. The personal encounters with war in Italy recorded in this book underscore the value of oral history in illuminating the frequently overlooked experiences of ordinary people caught up in war, and the range of reactions which different aspects of war evoked from them. As Gordon Johnston's case illustrates, these interviews remind us that combat — the quintessential war experience — was by no means the sole defining feature of New Zealand experiences in Italy during the Second World War. Instead, they highlight how the misery of war can paradoxically yield some positive outcomes, and how its sorrow can be lightened by certain ordinary, but humanly important, aspects of life.

The purpose of this introduction is to provide readers with a sense of the wider context in which those varied individual experiences were played out. It thus begins with a discussion of the broader strategic, diplomatic and political decisions which ensured that so many New Zealanders found themselves fighting in Italy, of all places, during the final two years of the Second World War. There is a brief narrative overview of the general military course of the campaign for the 2nd New Zealand Division. The introduction also draws on the personal memories in the following interviews to highlight some general themes in the experiences of the New Zealand citizen-soldiers who trudged up the long Italian *strada* ('road' or 'street') from Taranto to Trieste.

STRATEGY, DIPLOMACY
AND POLITICS

FROM LATE 1943 TO MID-1945, New Zealand's combat contribution to the Allied struggle against the Axis powers was concentrated primarily on the Italian peninsula. That so many New Zealanders found themselves fighting in this setting was a result of their government's response to Allied grand strategy in the Second World War. The decision to commit the country's major fighting force to this theatre was the New Zealand government's most controversial strategic decision of the war. It differed markedly from that of Australia, which drew back its forces to the Pacific theatre after the successful outcome of the Allied campaign in North Africa. Italy was thus the only significant theatre of conflict during the war where New Zealand soldiers did not fight alongside or near their Australian counterparts. Controversy about this commitment has continued to the present, with some historians, politicians and other commentators drawing unfavourable comparisons with Australia's action and inferring that the decision made in Wellington to remain in the Mediterranean theatre was a mark of subservience to Britain and demonstrated a singular lack of 'independence'.

The Allied decision to embark on an Italian campaign was itself a subject of controversy, uncertainty and debate at the highest levels. At the Casablanca Conference in January 1943, British Prime Minister Winston Churchill and American President Franklin D. Roosevelt agreed to exploit Allied military successes in North Africa by launching Mediterranean operations that would culminate in the invasion of Sicily (Operation Husky). Although British and American planners resolved at the Trident Conference in May that Operation Husky must remain secondary to a cross-channel invasion of France, they recognised that it might precipitate Italy's early elimination from the war. There was, however, Anglo-American disagreement concerning the extent to which an Italian campaign should be waged. Churchill vigorously pressed the case for attacking the 'soft underbelly of Europe'. Not only did an invasion of Italy offer the prospect of an early defeat for one of the three Axis powers; it could open the way for Allied operations in the Balkans, and Italian air bases could be used to augment the aerial bombing campaign against Germany. American strategists, however, criticised Churchill's 'strategic opportunism' and were wary about dissipating Allied energies, which they believed could be better focused on opening a second front in Western Europe, thereby responding to Joseph Stalin's demands for visible action to ease the Nazi pressures on the Eastern front. When Allied forces attacked Sicily on 10 July 1943, there was still uncertainty at the highest levels about where exactly they would move next. It was not until the Quebec Conference in the following month that definite American agreement to the invasion of Italy was secured, in large part because more time was needed to prepare for the opening of a second front in France.

By then Italy was nearing collapse. Two weeks after the first Allied landings on Sicily, the country's Fascist leader, Benito Mussolini, was overthrown in an internal coup, encouraging the Allies to proceed with a full-blown invasion of the mainland. The new Italian military government of General Pietro Badoglio immediately opened secret negotiations, which were to lead to Italy's surrender and withdrawal from the war on 8 September, less than a week after the Allies launched their assault on Italy proper, with a landing in the southern province of Calabria.

The repercussions of Italy's collapse were dramatic. Germany's Nazi leader, Adolf Hitler, acted quickly and decisively in response to this significant Allied victory. He ordered Field Marshal Albert Kesselring to use the eighteen German divisions that had been deployed in Italy in the preceding months to occupy the country. Under Kesselring's capable leadership, the Germans thereafter adopted an astute defensive strategy which took full advantage of Italy's topography and relatively narrow width. The first of these defensive lines was the so-called Gustav Line, established to the south of Rome to prevent an advance on the capital. The Germans also rescued Mussolini, who established a puppet regime known as the Fascist Republic of Salò, thereby ensuring that Italy became the setting for a civil war as well as a battlefield for foreign armies. This aspect of the conflict was formalised by the Italian government declaring war on Germany, which meant that Italian troops would end up fighting on both sides of the front line. To further complicate the situation, increasing numbers of Italians living in areas still under German occupation joined competing partisan groups which varied in ideological persuasion from communist to liberal-democratic.

The Italian armistice inaugurated a new phase in the Second World War: the beginning of a transition to the post-war era. As the first Axis power to surrender and experience Allied occupation, Italy became a critical testing ground for the unity of the anti-Nazi coalition and for Allied post-war planning. At the same time, much of the country remained an active war zone until a few days before the final Allied victory in Europe in May 1945. The Italian campaign thus became a political–military minefield, precipitating ongoing political tensions between the three major Allied powers. Roosevelt remarked to Churchill in October 1943 that Allied occupation policy in Italy would 'set the precedent for all such future activities in the war'. New Zealand would not be immune from the political dimensions of the Italian campaign, especially in the closing days of the European war, when its forces would become entangled in a possible showdown with those of an erstwhile ally, Yugoslavia.

The very question of participation in the Italian campaign was politically vexatious for the New Zealand government from the outset. Developments in the Mediterranean theatre of operations caused much agonising in Wellington from early 1943. The government turned down Churchill's request for New Zealand forces to contribute to the invasion of Sicily. But then in May 1943, Prime Minister Peter Fraser agreed that the 2nd Division would remain in Europe rather than emulating Australia's example of redeploying forces closer to home in the Pacific.

Superficially, this decision may seem to validate the criticism that New Zealand's wartime policy was subservient to British interests. It is true, for instance, that it led Winston Churchill to compare New Zealand leaders very favourably to their Australian counterparts, whom he described privately as having 'failed us'. There was, moreover, a general appreciation in London for New Zealand as the 'good boy of the Commonwealth family'. But Churchill and his advisers remained acutely aware that they could not take New Zealand for granted. They were at pains in 1943 to present sound military reasons for their request that New Zealand retain the 2nd Division in the Mediterranean theatre, and knew that the issue was being hotly debated in Wellington. As Churchill told his advisers, it was not a matter of 'testing New Zealand's loyalty', but of explaining the efficacy for the overall Allied cause of having the 2nd Division remain in the Mediterranean. In the end, the British were delighted with the outcome of the debate in Wellington, but they understood that the decision had been very much in the balance and that many domestic political concerns had had to be overcome in securing parliamentary approval not to bring the troops back to the Pacific theatre.

In fact, the Fraser government's decision was made with a keen appreciation of New Zealand's national interests. It was fully in line with the government's overarching wartime strategy, which was based on the recognition that, as a small state dependent on more powerful allies, what mattered most to New Zealand was how it could help secure victory for the Allied cause in the principal theatres of battle. That is why the decision was made in 1943, after lengthy deliberation and soul-searching debate, to retain the 2nd Division in the Mediterranean theatre, where the hard-won battle experience of its soldiers might best be utilised. Moreover, it avoided such practical problems as transporting the forces home and retraining them to fight in the decidedly different jungle environment of the Pacific theatre. This strategy did not always command universal support within New Zealand, and in 1943 there was considerable public pressure on the government to bring the 'boys' closer to home. But, though based on a different approach to that of Australia, this strategic decision was not necessarily any less 'independent' or heedless of national interests.

Even at the end of the Italian campaign, when an inter-Allied crisis arose concerning the city of Trieste, New Zealand's support for Britain was by no means automatic. Admittedly, Peter Fraser was quick to accede to Churchill's request in early May 1945 that the 2nd Division be used, if necessary, as part of a combat force to prevent a Yugoslav seizure of the disputed city. In Wellington, several Labour Cabinet members were uneasy about involvement in a potential confrontation with Yugoslav forces, and suspicious that Churchill was merely seeking to assert residual pretensions of British influence in Balkan affairs. Fraser, however, disagreed with some of his colleagues on this issue, not because he was seeking to please Churchill, but because he believed key principles were at stake in Trieste with respect to the more general challenge of assuring orderly territorial settlements in the aftermath of the war. Just as had been the case with respect to the Italian campaign, the Fraser government's stance on this issue was not based on acquiescence to British desires but was consistent with a broader strategic assumption that New Zealand's interests as a small country in the post-war world would best be served by supporting the evolution of a rule-based system of international order.

THE CAMPAIGN

THE CRUCIAL POLITICAL DECISION MADE in Wellington in 1943 ensured that the bulk of New Zealand's active soldiers would see action in Italy until the end of the war in Europe. While there, they would fight as part of (the soon-to-be-replaced) General Sir Bernard Montgomery's multinational Eighth Army, with which they had also been associated in the desert campaigns. For the New Zealanders of the 2nd Division, though, the only general who really mattered was their own commander, Lieutenant General Bernard Freyberg. 'Tiny' Freyberg was an able, energetic leader who held the hard-won respect of his men, in part because of his well-known concern for their wellbeing and his aversion to casualties.

The force that Freyberg would lead in Italy had been seasoned by two years of active warfare. With a strong sense of camaraderie forged in the heat of battle, New Zealand's predominantly amateur soldiers had transformed themselves into the Div — a formidable fighting force with a reputation for quiet but dogged efficiency. They had definitely acquitted themselves well in the deserts of North Africa, where they had fought since late 1941 after disheartening defeats and decampment from Greece and Crete. But they were not necessarily prepared for the conditions which they would encounter on the other side of the Mediterranean Sea.

Accordingly, after the decision was made to commit the New Zealand force to Italy, its members were allowed a period of recuperation and some months to reorganise in Egypt. Many of those who had served longest were permitted a furlough back home, and the 2nd Division was strengthened with reinforcements from New Zealand before setting off for Italy in October 1943. The new arrivals were fresh, but they were untested in battle and had yet to be integrated into the ways of the Div. Moreover, the seasoned soldiers who remained were as battle-weary as they were battle-hardened. Their first port of call was Taranto, then they moved on to assemble in Bari, which would serve thereafter as the main staging base for New Zealand troops arriving in Italy.

The Div was in action by the end of November. The New Zealanders were assigned the task of joining the Allied effort to breach the Gustav Line by attacking its eastern margins and crossing the Sangro River with the hope of initiating an advance to Rome. They made good initial progress, suffering about 150 casualties but capturing several hundred Germans and skilfully using Bailey bridges to ford the Sangro — one of a seemingly endless succession of rivers they would traverse in their long advance up the Italian peninsula. On 2 December, the Div secured the village of Castelfrentano — a place name memorialised in a popular song of the Italian campaign. They moved on to attack the town of Orsogna, and it even seemed possible that they would break through the Gustav Line. Although New Zealand infantry actually entered the town on 3 December, they were driven out by German reinforcements, bolstered by tanks. Despite repeated attacks in the succeeding weeks, the Germans proved immovable. With winter deepening, the whole Allied offensive ground to a halt, and spirits were low amongst the New Zealanders when they were finally withdrawn from the stalled front line in January 1944, after suffering some 1600 casualties during their first two months of combat in Italy.

The division was to enjoy only a brief respite before being called upon to participate in a new attack on a strongpoint that would prove the most tragically elusive prize of the entire campaign for the New Zealanders. They now moved across to the other side of Italy to join the Allied forces massing before the town of Cassino. The Germans' success in blunting the Allied offensive prompted an effort to push through the strategically pivotal Liri Valley and on to Rome. The problem was that the entrance to the valley was just over 10 kilometres wide and was overlooked by a monastery atop the 500-metre high Monte Cassino. Augmented by the Germans' meticulous deployment of minefields, fortifications, and flooding through the demolition of stopbanks, Cassino was a defender's dream and an attacking army's nightmare. New Zealand involvement in this challenging task was in part due to the failure of the

American Fifth Army's assault on Anzio in a seaborne attack intended to bypass the German front line.

Temporarily commanding a New Zealand Corps bolstered by the inclusion of the 4th Indian Division, Freyberg now steeled himself and his forces for the battle ahead. Desperate to minimise casualties, he requested that a massive bombardment of the German defences precede the assault by his troops. Approved by the Supreme Allied Commander in the Mediterranean himself, General Sir Harold Alexander, the subsequent aerial bombardment on 15 February laid waste the historic monastery and its environs. Controversy about this decision would persist long after the war was over — the Germans vehemently denied that they had occupied the monastery. But, tragically for the waiting New Zealand soldiers, they were able to exploit the ruins to create an even more formidable set of defences.

Freyberg nevertheless proceeded with the plan, which involved the Indian Division attacking Cassino from the north, while the New Zealanders attacked from the south with the hope of punching an opening into the Liri Valley. It fell to 28 (Maori) Battalion to initiate the attack on the town's well-defended railway station on 17 February. After one of the fiercest and costliest battles in the annals of this legendary unit, the battalion seized positions in and around the station. But the equally courageous engineers behind them were thwarted in their efforts to clear a path through the flooded terrain for support weapons. Without these weapons, the isolated Maori soldiers were forced to withdraw after a counterattack by German infantry backed by tanks. It was the first of numerous bitter disappointments for the New Zealanders at Cassino.

A series of other brave but unsuccessful assaults ensued. After another heavy bombardment, New Zealand forces fought their way into the devastated town on 15 March. Once again, the Germans put up tenacious resistance from hidden positions in the maze of rubble that was once Cassino. After eight days of fighting, Freyberg decided the cost was proving too high and ordered his troops to cease their advance. Shortly afterwards, in early April, the New Zealand Division withdrew from the Cassino area, having suffered almost 350 deaths and many more wounded.

Cassino did not eventually fall until May, to British and Polish troops supported by New Zealand artillery. The Gustav Line was finally breached, and Allied forces entered Rome on 4 June, two days before D-Day. The success of the cross-channel invasion meant that the Italian campaign became an undeniably secondary theatre of operations, with seven Allied divisions redeployed to France in August. The Italian campaign's main purpose was now to divert part of the German war effort by tying down forces which might otherwise have been used to defend France and Germany itself.

After a period of rest and recuperation, the Div was back in action again in July as part of the Allied effort to breach the Germans' new 'Gothic Line', which ran across the northern Apennines from Pisa to Rimini. The New Zealanders enjoyed early success in their return to the battlefield, capturing the town of Arezzo on 16 July. Seeking to move on to Florence, they encountered solid German resistance before reaching the city on 4 August. They were back in the line the following month, fighting their way across difficult terrain in a slow advance to the east of the mountains, which brought them to the Savio

River by the end of October. They now had a month's break during which the division was reorganised.

They rejoined the attack in late November and captured Faenza on 15 December. Having reached the Senio River, the division halted and endured its second Italian winter. After another period of relief, the Div lined up again on the banks of the Senio River on 8 April to begin what would prove the final offensive in Italy. The New Zealanders now moved forward at an increasingly rapid pace. After crossing the Senio, the drive continued to the Santerno River and then on to the Gaiana. Briefly halted there, the New Zealanders then pushed on to the Idice before crossing the Po River on Anzac Day. Taking Padua on 28 April, the Div embarked on its last helter-skelter advance, amidst disintegrating German resistance and with partisan successes everywhere.

The Div crossed the Isonzo River on 1 May and reached Trieste the next day, just as the German forces in Italy surrendered unconditionally. After an exhilarating final charge, during which they had covered more than 220 kilometres in less than a week, the New Zealanders arrived just in time to share in the city's liberation with local partisans and units of Josip Tito's Fourth Yugoslav Army. It should have been a final moment of glory in the Italian campaign — a chance to savour the end of the war in Europe and relax before a speedy return home. Instead, it proved a 'helluva way to end a war', as one soldier recorded in his diary. The fortunes of war had pitched the Div into an international hot spot, as Trieste became the setting for the first inter-Allied clash in post-war Europe.

The city was the focal point of a bitter territorial dispute between Italy and Yugoslavia. The Yugoslavs had hoped to strengthen their post-war claims to Trieste by being first to liberate it and then putting in place their own military administration. The Western Allies, however, had planned that the city should come under Allied Military Government like other parts of liberated Italy, pending a final peace settlement. By arriving in Trieste when they did, the 2nd Division dashed the Yugoslavs' hopes of presenting the Western Allies with a *fait accompli*. For some weeks, Trieste was under an uneasy dual occupation. Only after the problem was resolved diplomatically at the highest Allied levels were the New Zealand soldiers able to relax. The Yugoslavs reluctantly withdrew from the city in mid-June.

The following month, the division began moving to Lake Trasimene in central Italy, from where most of the New Zealanders would begin their long journey home. Limited availability of shipping meant that this was a slow process, and it was not until February 1946 that the last members of the Div ended their wartime Italian sojourn.

EXPERIENCES REMEMBERED

WAR CREATES A HIGHLY UNUSUAL context for human behaviour, unsettling social norms, morality, and the very rules of human survival. For soldiers themselves, war is very much about 'killing time' in two senses. On the one hand, it entails periods of time in combat — mercifully brief, for the most part — which are experienced in life-threatening form, with an adrenaline-charged intensity and far removed from everything that passes for normal life. On the other, it is about enduring extended periods of boredom, ostensibly involving preparation for battle but also filled with other preoccupations, most of which are the stuff of everyday life. For many, such as New Zealand's citizen soldiers, war also represents a punctuation in the normal progression of life during which career development, romance, family life, socialising in one's home surroundings and the like are all put on hold — with the added possibility of returning home maimed physically or psychologically, or not at all.

The varied New Zealand memories in this book confirm that the Italian campaign was no exception as far as these general effects of war are concerned. These interviews highlight the human impact of the diplomatic, strategic and military developments summarised in the preceding sections. Although they reveal that the New Zealand experience in Italy from 1943 to 1945 involved more than war, combat itself was the most intense of the experiences confronted. After all, armies are assembled for fighting, and never more so than when they consist of ordinary citizens called to arms during wartime. The 2nd Division was precisely such a force. In fact, 65 years on, the remaining Italian campaign veterans are amongst the few New Zealanders who have experienced battle on a grand scale and on a widespread generational basis.

Not all the interviewees in this book engaged in combat at first hand, but all felt its effects in one way or another during their time in Italy. It was most searing for those who were front-line troops. Amongst those, Gordon Slatter's recollections of combat are the most reflective, in part perhaps because he was the author of several books based on his wartime experience in Italy. His general observations about how he responded to the unique pressures of battle have an arresting universality about them: 'I was frightened most of the time but sometimes, for some unknown reason, I got quite brave, and I still don't know why.' His candid confession that 'I came away from the war as puzzled about it as when I went' succinctly evokes the enduring mystery of war. The sheer arbitrariness of death or survival in battle is encapsulated in Slatter's almost off-hand conclusion that 'It was all a matter of luck, I suppose'. This arbitrariness also features prominently in the recollections of Reg Hermans, whose matter-of-fact account of his own efforts as an engineer engaged in bridge-building — a crucial task in a country with so many rivers to cross — belies the heroism which won him a Military Cross. Driven by the goal 'to get home in one piece', Hermans did return, but only after being badly wounded.

As in all armies, not every New Zealand soldier responded to the challenges of combat with heroism. Rae Familton recalls that the cruelty of war can have other consequences, and his account of the after effects of trauma felt by one tank driver represents countless such occurrences. As he stresses, the driver 'wasn't a coward. It was just that his nervous system couldn't take the effects of being hit in his tank'. Interestingly, Familton suggests that the view taken towards such incidents was very different from that during the First World War, for 'if anything like that happened' in Italy, 'it was handed straight over to the medical people', not to the military police.

Cassino remains the source of some of the most bitter memories of combat in Italy. Familton still remembers the sight of 600 bombers attacking the monastery at Monte Cassino: 'It was a beautiful day and you could see the detonations travelling through the air.' There was also the matter of coping with dead and dying men all around them at close quarters. Several interviewees comment on this, with Joseph Bacos recalling that 'The stench of the rotting bodies is something I can still smell in my nostrils.' Ironically, Cassino may feature so prominently in New Zealand memories of the Italian campaign because it represented a costly failure.

In general, though, there is a clear pride in the military performance of New Zealand's citizen-soldiers running through the recollections in this book. For Slatter, much of this perceived success was due to the egalitarian spirit which infused the ethos of the Div and, in particular, the way in which respect for officers was founded on performance: 'When I was there, sergeants and corporals didn't sew on stripes. They led. You knew who they were, and you followed them.' Slatter articulates a commonly held view in his judgement that the division 'was so formidable because of that feeling between the ranks and the concern for each other'. This concern on the part of officers is well exemplified in Familton's tragic account of trying to avoid the death of a third young man from a single Balclutha family. The strong sense of solidarity so often forged at the small-unit level in successful armies appears to have manifested itself more widely within the Div, perhaps fortified by underlying notions of 'mateship'. In the case of 28 (Maori) Battalion, Tini Glover reflects that group solidarity was even stronger, for 'blood is thicker than water'; the Maori soldiers were 'so good because we fought in blood lots'.

Although most New Zealanders who fought in Italy were members of the 2nd Division, hundreds served in other ways. A significant number of New Zealand pilots served in the Royal Air Force. They flew fighters and fighter-bombers in support of armies on the ground, and strategic bombing missions from bases in Italy — the control of these bases being arguably the most militarily significant achievement of the Italian campaign for the overall Allied cause. Some New Zealanders served in the Fleet Air Arm — men like Douglas Park, whose recollections of that experience are included in this book. Others, like Joseph Pedersen, saw action off the coast of Italy as seamen in British warships. As Pedersen mentions in passing, there was also another category of New Zealand combatant in Italy — escaped prisoners of war who joined Italian partisan bands to engage in guerrilla warfare against the Germans.

For those who did serve on the ground with the Div, the distinctive topographical and climatic conditions that they encountered figure prominently in their memories of military experience in Italy. The country in which they arrived in 1943 constituted a very different battlefield from the desert landscape which they had just left. The terrain was mountainous and varied, in contrast to the sand-covered sameness of much of North Africa — conditions which created an ideal defensive situation for their German foes. As Joseph Bacos points out, such conditions were not suited to tanks and hampered the warfare of mobility at which the New Zealanders had proved themselves so adept in the desert. Moreover, the weather also presented challenges, with the stock image of 'sunny Italy' seeming more like a desert mirage in the winters of 1943–45. Instead, in the words of Patricia Hamilton, a Tui: 'It was cold, and it was a different sort of war — mud and snow and slush.' The mud was especially memorable for those who struggled through it on foot or in vehicles. At the end of the conflict, however, the more benign aspects of Italy's climate and topography would be enjoyed as the members of the 2nd

Division took full advantage of the recreational opportunities afforded by an Adriatic summer — whose pleasures were no doubt heightened by the knowledge that the European war was over.

Another difference between the combat experience in the North African desert and in Italy was the more sustained and extensive encounters with the local population. Italy's anomalous status as a former foe now formally fighting alongside the Allies may have puzzled some soldiers. But most merely focused on the Italians as ordinary people who were victims of war and who generally welcomed them. As Gordon Johnston stresses, there was much sympathy amongst the New Zealanders for Italians who suffered, especially the children. There was also much admiration for Italian women — and not simply on the basis of sexual attraction — but less respect for Italian men. Many New Zealanders were aware of Italy's rich cultural heritage, which may have influenced their views of the local populace. In general, the New Zealanders found themselves constantly engaging in cross-cultural encounters matching the military ones that confronted them whenever they were 'off up the strada' — an expression repeated often amongst the troops, as Slatter notes. Indeed, one of the most colourful manifestations of the impact of these cross-cultural encounters was the widespread incorporation of bastardised Italian expressions in the distinctive argot of the Div — a singularly appropriate development in a country with so many different local dialects. For example, as Reginald Minter points out, once in Italy, New Zealanders invariably referred to their German adversaries as 'Ted' or 'the Teds', an abbreviation of Tedeschi, the Italian word for 'Germans'. (In fact, there was considerable respect for the Germans as soldiers — a respect which appeared to have been reciprocated.)

There is also much in these interviews about the non-combat experiences, which occupied a high proportion of the time spent by New Zealanders during the Italian campaign. Touring is recalled by many interviewees as an activity they engaged in whenever possible. It was one of the ironies of war that fighting in Italy exposed thousands of New Zealanders who would have not otherwise been able to venture anywhere near Europe to one of the world's great cultures.

Not all the activities pursued by New Zealanders when not in combat were as wholesome as seeing the sights or attending operas. In an era when 'rugby, racing and beer' defined so much about male popular culture in New Zealand, it is not surprising that gambling (often linked to sports events) and drinking were welcome distractions from war for many soldiers. Looting was another popular New Zealand pursuit in Italy, with some believing that the Div was well deserving of the epithet of 'Freyberg and his forty thousand thieves'. Opinions continue to differ as to its extent. Johnston believes that it was limited in scale, in part because of limited opportunities for a combat force which spent little time in Italy's larger cities. Moreover, much of the looting that did occur was said to have targeted the homes and possessions of wealthier Italians, most of whom were Fascist sympathisers, rather than the simple peasants with whom the New Zealanders usually interacted. Isobelle Wright, however, recalls enthusiastic New Zealand participation in black-market activities. Perhaps because she was based in Rome, her recollection is that New Zealanders 'were noted for their looting' and 'pretty good at it'. Some

'Maori boys' even offered to get her a car, for 'nothing was a trouble'. Tini Glover's recollections confirm the entrepreneurial zeal with which members of the Maori Battalion went about accumulating items such as German Lugers for subsequent sale to less enterprising but richer American soldiers. But within the Div, looting was by no means a Maori monopoly. Even Jack Somerville, then a chaplain and subsequently one of New Zealand's most distinguished churchmen, admits that in the ruins at Cassino, he 'managed to snaffle a book which is in the Knox College library now'.

Wright is one of two women whose interviews offer a female perspective on the Italian campaign. As a nurse, she saw the full consequences of what war did to men. She still remembers the screams of men having nightmares, but notes, 'They wouldn't admit to being nervous once you wakened them and quietened them down. They wouldn't say they were scared or overworked. They never complained. That was the difference between them and the English army.' The other female interviewee, Pat Hamilton, was a Tui. The Tuis worked in the New Zealand servicemen's club, in Bari at first and later in Rome. Their duties included serving food and drinks, visiting injured soldiers in hospital, writing letters for disabled soldiers and packing POW packages. Hamilton met her husband, Peter, at Bari. Her account of their wedding arrangements shows how human kindness can thrive under the most inauspicious circumstances. Wright, too, was married during war in Italy, providing another example of romance blossoming in wartime. As Gordon and Luciana Johnston found, it can even transcend barriers of language.

Alongside romance and marriage, there were sexual liaisons

of a less lasting kind. Even though wartime conditions are not conducive to forming longer-term relationships, it is not surprising that sexual abstinence is far from the norm whenever armies move through a country in which they find themselves in close proximity to civilians. Recorded rates of venereal diseases within the 2nd Division leave no doubt that many New Zealanders visited prostitutes. Such visits amounted to sexual initiation rites for some young men, as Tini Glover recounts with humour with respect to one 'young joker'. Short-term affairs with local Italian women also occurred in some cases. There probably were homosexual liaisons too, but, reflecting the social mores of the time, that taboo subject is not usually mentioned in recorded memories of the Italian campaign.

Taken together, the interviews do hint at a distinctive New Zealand national identity manifesting itself in Italy. Amongst its more noteworthy qualities were egalitarianism, irreverence, and an easy-going, pragmatic approach to soldiering and life. A bicultural dimension was also present, although this was often understated and at times a source of tension, as is suggested in Tini Glover's allusions to the use of the word 'Hori'. There was a clear aversion to hierarchy, authority, military formalities and 'skiting' within the Div, and an equally clear respect for achievement by both officers and other ranks. Alongside a self-deprecating style of humour, there was also a laconically expressed but deeply felt confidence amongst the New Zealanders that they represented one of the best countries in the world. Fighting together with so many of their countrymen in Italy for a sustained period of time, and jostling against other national groups, both friends and foes, helped strengthen that sense of 'New Zealand-ness' for the soldiers of the 2nd Division.

This reinforcement of an implicit national self-consciousness is well captured in a comment by Joseph Bacos about how the campaign 'broadened one's outlook tremendously', for 'coming from a little country in the South Pacific and seeing the northern hemisphere and how other people lived' served to heighten his awareness of 'how lucky we are here'.

MEANINGS

THE INTERVIEWS IN THIS BOOK suggest that, for those New Zealanders who fought in Italy, the war had many meanings. For men and women like Johnston, Wright and Hamilton, their memories of it will be forever coloured by the personal happiness associated with their joyful association with life-long partners. Admittedly, even for them, it remains tinged with the sort of sorrow which Pat Hamilton's husband felt at the war's end in remembering 'all the boys that he had known and liked so much who were not celebrating it with him'. Nevertheless, it is striking how so many of those interviewed for this volume regard the personal impact of their wartime experience in Italy in positive terms. Joseph Bacos, Newton Wickham and Reginald Minter, for example, all mention that it was definitely a memorable adventure, with Minter concluding, 'I wouldn't have missed it for quids.'

Collectively, the experience may be assessed in other ways. Militarily, New Zealand had contributed to a campaign that some came to dismiss as a sideshow. But it did serve to hold down German forces which Hitler could have used on the Eastern front, and later to counter the Allied landings in France.

For New Zealand the cost of the deployment in Italy was high. Nearly 9000 casualties were suffered, including 2003 deaths. But it served New Zealand's overall strategic objectives well by making a highly visible and nationally distinctive contribution to the prosecution of the war in Europe.

Perhaps, however, the larger significance of the Italian campaign for New Zealanders may best be explained in other terms. On one level at least, the 2nd Division's experience in Italy could be seen as a general vindication not only of New Zealand's achievements in the Second World War, but of its successful development as a nation. When the New Zealanders left Trieste, a local newspaper farewelled them with these words:

> *They have shown us that there still exists one country in the world where society does not corrupt the individual but makes him more thoughtful toward his fellow men ... Goodbye, our New Zealand brothers ... perhaps because we are so fond of you — we are pleased that you are leaving us to return to your own healthy country and that you are going away from this old and sick place which is called Europe, which if you had to stay here would infect you with all its evil.*

It was a moving tribute to suggest that New Zealand stood as this sort of symbolic as well as geographical antipode to the old and corrupt European world. Although most of the soldiers to whom those words were addressed would have been too modest to admit it, the national self-image evoked in that commentary was one which they would have readily accepted. In that sense, the Italian campaign served as reassuring confirmation for the soldiers of the 2nd Division of a commitment to the principles of fair play which they liked to think their nation represented, and which endowed their war effort with evident pride. More than six decades on, that legacy continues to merit respectful commemoration as part of the larger meaning of New Zealand's participation in the Italian campaign.

FURTHER READING

The land campaign in Italy is covered in two volumes of the *Official History of New Zealand in the Second World War* published by the War History Branch of the Department of Internal Affairs: N.C. Phillips, *Italy, Volume I, The Sangro to Cassino* (1957), and Robin Kay, *Italy, Volume II, From Cassino to Trieste* (1967). Activities of New Zealanders in the RAF are described in H.L. Thompson, *New Zealanders in the Royal Air Force, Volume III* (1959). S.D. Waters, *Royal New Zealand Navy* (1956), records the efforts of some of the New Zealanders who served with the Royal Navy in the Mediterranean during the campaign. Various aspects of the campaign are also covered in Ian McGibbon (ed.), *The Oxford Companion to New Zealand Military History* (2000). Matthew Wright, *Italian Odyssey: New Zealanders in the Battle for Italy 1943–45*, provides a recent short history of the campaign; and Susan Jacobs, *Fighting with the Enemy: New Zealand POWs and the Italian Resistance* (2003), covers the role of New Zealand POWs who fought with the Italians. Biographies of participants, ranging from divisional commander to escaped POW turned saboteur, include Paul Freyberg, *Bernard Freyberg V.C., Soldier of Two Nations* (1991); Laurie Barber and John Tonkin-Covell, *Freyberg: Churchill's Salamander* (1989); Glyn Harper, *Kippenberger, An Inspired New Zealand Commander* (1997); Denis McLean, *Kippenberger: The Gift of Leadership* (2008); and Florence N. Millar, *The 'Signor Kiwi' Saga* (1993). There are numerous accounts by participants ranging in rank from major general to private, including Major General Sir Howard Kippenberger, *Infantry Brigadier* (1949); Geoffrey Cox, *The Race to Trieste* (1977); Arch Scott, *Dark of the Moon* (1985); Sgt L.H. (Shorty) Lovegrove, *Cavalry? You Mean*

Horses (1994); Pat Kane, *A Soldier's Story: A Mediterranean Odyssey* (1995); Gordon Slatter, *One More River: The Final Campaign of the Second New Zealand Division in Italy* (1995); Leslie Hobbs, *Kiwi Down the Strada* (1963); and Roger Smith, *Up the Blue: A Kiwi Private's View of the Second World War* (2000).

'THE GOOD OLD AGE
OF SEVENTEEN'

Joseph PEDERSEN, RNZN 2337, Able Seaman, Royal New Zealand Navy

Joseph Pedersen's paternal grandparents were Norwegians who were among the original settlers of Norsewood in southern Hawke's Bay. Joseph was born in Palmerston North in October 1923. His mother, Alice, died when he was seven years of age and the family moved back to Norsewood where his father, Herbert, farmed. After leaving Dannevirke High School at the end of 1939, Joseph worked for the railways in Napier for three months before joining the navy.

As OTHER YOUNG MEN WHO had enlisted in the army left Napier by train, the railway workers would blow all the whistles while the train was going out. I joined up from there. I thought, I've got to be a hero too.

Was that because the navy would take you at seventeen?
Yes. The navy or the air force. I couldn't go in the army, but they did take young people in the navy. They took them from fifteen and a half, so I applied and I went straight in.

How did your father feel about you joining up?

He was quite happy. I went down to Norsewood and got him to sign the paper and posted it away. He didn't want me to go in the army after he'd been at Gallipoli and in France. He'd been four years over there. He got wounded two or three times. He got gassed there and used to cough and splutter. It affected him right through until he died.

I didn't have to do anything, except have a medical. From Napier they sent me a rail ticket to report to HMS *Philomel* [in Auckland] and I went up there and had a medical and all the tests, and stayed from that point on. I was in the navy. You had to march round on a parade ground for about three months with a rifle and pretend you knew what to do.

They issued me with naval clothes — shorts. They called them 'Bombay bloomers', and they came down past your knees. You could wrap them around your stomach about three times. You had your blues and your white hat and your dickies, as they called them — those are the white things that go around your neck. They gave you everything. Shoes, socks, hammock. I used to love my hammock. In fact, I think it's the best bed I ever had.

I did my training, then I went on a troopship through the Panama Canal and arrived in the middle of an air raid in Cardiff. There were about 100 naval personnel and about 50 Free French sailors from Tahiti. We'd called in at Kingston in Jamaica and dashed across the Atlantic, by ourselves. It was a fast ship — it did about eighteen knots. It was a good ship, but it got sunk off Algiers.

Joseph joined the New Zealand Division of the Royal Navy, but while in England he received a letter

*explaining that he was now part of the Royal New
Zealand Navy, which the division was redesignated
in 1941. About half of the men he had joined up
with had been posted to New Zealand ships, while
he and the rest were sent to England to join Royal
Navy ships. He joined at the lowest rank, ordinary
seaman.*

You couldn't be [lower than my rank], other than a seaman boy.
You had to be fifteen for that. I had to wait till I was eighteen
before they made me an able seaman.

After [landing at] Cardiff, we went by train down to
Devonport. When we got there, there were air raids and the
New Zealand 'Rockies' (RNVR guys who'd gone over in October
1940) were on strike because of the lousy food that the naval
barracks was dishing up to the New Zealanders. There were
about a hundred of them. They refused to do any duties, so they
rang up the High Commissioner, [William] Jordan, in London,
and he came down and stirred the Admiralty up. We arrived
in the middle of that.

We never did any duties, because they put us down in
Nissen huts at the far end of the parade ground and had nothing
to do with us. I was there for about six weeks and then I went
up to Scotland and did my ASDIC training in a place called
Dunoon, at HMS *Osprey*. Then I joined the destroyer HMS
Walker, in Liverpool.

You volunteered for what you wanted to do. A lot of our
guys went into the torpedo school, others wanted to be gunners.
I didn't. I went up to Scotland, and I'm pleased I did because
I loved Scotland. The ASDIC training took three months. Later

on they called it sonar. You had to do electrical theory and you had to be quite good at distinguishing sound. You sent out beams and found any obstruction out in the sea and you had to pick out the different sounds. It was very high-pitched sound. I passed that all right, there was no problem there. It was good, I enjoyed it.

Because I was an ASDIC rating, I had to go on convoy duty. I just happened to pick an old dump of a destroyer. We'd do six weeks at sea one way; we'd go Liverpool to Londonderry usually, or Belfast, then up to Reykjavik in Iceland, or sometimes we'd go round Greenland, down the Denmark Strait. We'd do about six weeks out there and then we'd stop at Reykjavik. We'd change convoys and then we'd go down to St John's in Newfoundland. And then from there we'd go to Halifax in Nova Scotia. We did that for a while. We'd be at sea for nearly three months. But then, later on, just before we came back to England, we were going from Halifax to a place called Sydney in Cape Breton Island. And then we'd go to Boston, and down to New York. I think we did four trips down there. We'd call in at Boston and spend four or five days there. Then spend four or five days in New York and come back again. Then we went back over to Liverpool, round to London and got home, and they decommissioned the ship. I was pleased to get off it. I hated the bloody thing.

On the North Atlantic convoys there would be five or six destroyers, including the American four-funnel destroyers. There were two of them in our group. We were the junior destroyer in the fleet, and we were usually at the tail of the convoy. We'd do the six-knot convoys, all the slow convoys — all the coal-burning convoys, where they fired their boilers with coal.

There'd be a cloud of black smoke over the whole convoy. Sometimes we'd get a report of a submarine so we'd be sent back to try and find it. You'd be on the horizon — you couldn't see the convoy but you could see the smoke cloud. Bloody cloud. No wonder the submarine could see us.

One of the old trawlers would be slow in the convoy, and we'd be sent back to hurry it along and we used to get the fingers sign: go to hell! They couldn't go any faster anyway. You just had to do your best. We lost quite a few of those sort of ships. No troopships or tankers, though once we had a submarine come right in the middle of the convoy and blow everything to bits. He shot off all his torpedoes, dived and was gone.

On the night of 16 March 1941, the convoy was attacked by a pack of German submarines.

We had a convoy of about 40 ships, I suppose, and it was about eleven o'clock at night. There were two operators on the watch. We picked up a signal, an echo sound. We had a button to push to tell the bridge we'd got an echo and it could be a submarine. So we did that and they said, 'Action stations'. And my boss, the Leading ASDIC rating — this guy got the DSM — came in and took over the operation. In action stations I was relieved of ASDICs because I was the most junior guy there and my action station was in B turret magazine, seven decks down. They never fired the gun all night. And boom! Boom! Under water you get depth charges dropping around everywhere from the destroyer escorts. We just sat there and listened to all the booming. There were five of us in the magazine. I'm a Catholic and I was saying my bloody prayers, ten to the dozen. These

47

other guys reckoned they were atheists. They said, 'No, we don't believe in God.' I believe every one of them was on his knees praying with me!

There were five submarines around and we brought one to the surface — I didn't know this till the next day. When I got up on deck the next day, I found we'd brought *U-99* to the surface, and we had about 40 German prisoners of war on the ship. We brought another ship, *U-100*, to the surface and then a sister ship, HMS *Vanoc*, rammed it. I believe we lost eleven ships that night, but between us we got two submarines. That was at the good old age of seventeen.

Depth charges put the submarine out of commission and they had to surface, and sink the ship. They all abandoned ship and we picked them up. They just walked around as though they were pleased to be out of the war. Most of them could speak good English. They were all nice guys and they were all pleased to be out of the war. In fact, I gave some of them some of my clean clothes because they had to chuck theirs away [as] they were covered in oil and what-have-you. I gave some of them my underclothes, and my warm jerseys and shirts. They just hopped around on the ship till we dropped them back at Liverpool. It took about 21 days to get them back. They didn't interfere, or even try to interfere. I had nothing to do with the [commanding] officer, of course. Otto Kretschmer was his name. He was quite free to walk around. You couldn't escort them because you had to do your duties.

I liked the navy and liked the fellowship of the navy, but I didn't like the *Walker* because I couldn't get clean on it. I was cold and miserable. It was a 1917 V & W series destroyer, from the First World War. It had no facilities on it at all, and you couldn't wash yourself, you couldn't have a shower, you couldn't have a bath. Cold water. Cork ceilings. It used to have icicles and they'd drip water on you all the time while you were supposed to be asleep. It was so bloody cold. And the seas were monstrous. I didn't like the North Atlantic at all. Hated it. But I got used to the seas in the North Atlantic and then when we did the landing in Sicily, they said the sea was very heavy and rough. There was a heavy swell, but I thought, this is just calm water after what I've been used to.

You'd wear your normal New Zealand woollen underclothes. Wool singlets that came down your arms. On top of that they gave you this thing like a boiler suit and it went right up round your neck and right down to your feet. There was a flap in the back. It had a fly. Then you'd put on your roll-neck jersey — and they were full length — and then you'd have your balaclava over your head and tied round your neck. Then on top of that you'd put your duffel coat. It was a thick coat with wooden buttons. And you wore that all the time. You never took it off the whole six weeks you were there. We found that the New Zealand Red Cross would send us over some woollen stockings. They were about half an inch thick and they went from your feet right up to your thigh. You had those on as well as your normal socks, plus all this other gear, and you were frozen. You were so bloody cold. You'd have your sea boots as well. When you got into your hammock at night, you'd only take off your sea boots. You didn't take off anything else.

Along the starboard side where you came in off the fo'c's'le, you'd go along and there was a cupboard along the side that had about eight aluminium basins which had a cold tap over them. There was no hot water. You had a dhobi [washing] bucket and a steam pipe on the back wall, and you'd get a bucket of warm water and pull the steam pipe into the bucket and heat the water up. Then you'd just wash your hands and your fingers and your nails, and your face. That's all you did. For six weeks. You couldn't smell the others because you smelled worse than what they did. Terrible bloody ship.

I wasn't old enough to get the rum ration.

After they decommissioned Walker, *what happened?*
I went back to the naval barracks in Dunoon, HMS *Osprey*, and I was there for a little while, and then they sent me on HMS *Royal Arthur* or *Royal Albert*, something like that. I went out and landed in Algiers. This was about June or July 1942.

> *In Algiers, Joseph was supposed to join the destroyer*
> *HMS* Lookout.

The destroyer wasn't in and I went into the barracks, HMS *Hannibal*, which was an ex-sultan's palace. From there I went each day and worked on the docks in a clothing store. There was an ammunition ship tied up at the docks, and alongside was HMS *Arrow*, an English destroyer. The Jerries came over at three o'clock in the afternoon and bombed this ship. Blew 50 metres of the wharf away, and all the superstructure of HMS *Arrow* just disappeared. It flattened the building I was in. I got caught under all the rubbish. I was covered in blankets until they dug me out next day. I was there about 18 hours, something like that. I was half unconscious [at first], but then I was all right, good as gold, but I found I was deaf and I couldn't hear. There was blood running out of my ears and my nose and my mouth. It was from the blast. I was lucky that I happened to be in the clothing store. They had a sick bay in HMS *Hannibal* and I was there six weeks.

When the destroyer came in, I joined the *Lookout*. It was a 1941 or 1942 destroyer. It was a year old, I think, when I joined it, and it had all the facilities — ventilation right through the ship, proper toilet and washing facilities, and a bit of space. Not only that, you were in a warmer climate. Beautiful sea, the Mediterranean. You'd be going along at night and the phosphorus would come out. It was beautiful. I used to stand and watch it when I was off watch. Beautiful.

It was a different ship altogether. Instead of a single four-inch gun, it had twin turrets, forward and aft, and they'd go right up at a 90-degree angle, so you could use them against aircraft. And they had ammunition hoists and things like that. I was a senior ASDIC rating then and my action station was on the ASDIC set. I didn't have much to do really, because when you were on convoy, escorting cruisers or battleships or carriers, or shelling along the coast, you'd be doing high speeds and you couldn't operate the ASDIC set at high speeds. The ship was twice as fast [as *Walker*], it could do 40 knots. So all I had to do was sit at the ASDIC set, which was on the bridge. When they weren't using the ASDICs, I used to stand on the port side of the bridge, right at the very back, out of the skipper's road, and act as an extra lookout. I stood there and watched all the action. All the landings in Sicily, all the shelling all along the coast, scraps with the E-boats — I just stood there and looked at it.

We'd go up as far as Cape Bon [in Tunisia], and we'd come back. We were following the American First Army along, shelling the coast. Off Cape Bon and in the Messina Straits, off the coast of Sicily, we'd run into E-boats. They're like motor torpedo boats, and they carry torpedoes. Radar couldn't pick them up — they were very low on the water. You could just pick them up on the ASDIC set. I could hear their motors just faintly. I'd say to the skipper, 'I think there's E-boats ahead, sir', so they'd call action stations and sure enough, we'd get up there a bit closer and there'd be four or five of them. They do about 45, 48 knots. They were very fast. One of our L-class destroyers off Cape Bon got hit by a motor torpedo boat. In North Africa and Italy the motor gunboats used to tie alongside us. They'd go right into the beaches, in between the islands, and have fights with these motor torpedo boats. They'd come back all shot up and with a few dead, but fortunately we weren't involved in it.

Lampedusa and Pantelleria are small Italian islands between Tunisia and Sicily.

We shelled Pantelleria for four days and our jimmy-the-one went ashore in a rowboat and took the surrender of the island. And then, I think the Coldstream Guards came in — there were about 50 of them. They took over from the Italian army there, it was a couple of thousand-strong, and our guys came back. Then we went on to Lampedusa. The whole fleet was there and we surrounded the harbour and just shelled it. The bombers were coming over and pattern-bombing. They were American bombers and they came over in waves of a hundred, right from the horizon. A hundred would come over and they'd drop their bombs there, and the next hundred would come over and they'd drop their bombs there. I'd say there'd be about a thousand aircraft over the period of time, dropping bombs, and we were shelling at the same time. Four days I did that. [The noise] didn't worry me. I was half deaf anyway. They surrendered straight away. Then the fleet buggered off to Malta and left us, and we had to patrol the island. That's when we got bombed. Bombers came over from Sicily to bomb the fleet and we were the only one there.

When [the Germans] were dive-bombing us off Lampedusa, I could see a dive-bomber coming. I could actually see the bomb coming. The skipper was sitting on the binnacle, on the upper deck, with his head back, and called, 'Hard aport!' He could see the bomb leave the plane, and he knew where it was going to hit so he was going [the other] way. We were the only ship there and they dive-bombed us for about 35 minutes, and they missed. Some of the boys on the aft deck got a bit of shrapnel.

It's funny. About eight o'clock at night you used to get William Joyce, Lord Haw Haw, [on the German radio] and later on [that] night after it had all finished, he said, 'Off Pantelleria today we sank G-32, HMS *Lookout*, with our dive-bombers.' We said, 'You've got it wrong this time, mate.' They never even hit us.

Then we went back to Malta and were tied up in Sliema Creek. There'd be several destroyers in there, all fleet destroyers, and they used to have swimming races. They'd put the boom out and lower the boats, and then between the destroyers you'd have swimming races and water polo. There were five Kiwis on the ship. I think there's seven in a water polo team and the five Kiwis were in the team. They were the only ones who could swim. And two Scotsmen. We used to swim against the other destroyers' crews. Nearly all of them couldn't swim. They wouldn't go in the water.

I used to walk out on the boom in Sliema Creek — beautiful. Lovely warm water, and I'd walk out on the boom which was twenty foot high, I suppose, and dive off into the sea. It was beautiful. The bombing had more or less finished in Malta because they were bombing Sicily then from Tunis, from aerodromes there.

From Malta we used to go up to the Messina Straits between Sicily and Italy. We engaged E-boats up there sometimes. Other times we'd go all the way to Taranto. We'd leave at about three o'clock in the afternoon, arrive at Taranto at about midnight, and then we'd just shell. There'd be three cruisers and about six or seven destroyers, and we'd just shell. I used to stand there and watch the trace shells. They'd shell for about two hours into Taranto. Two or three times we did that, and each time we were there, there was always an oil tank or something like that blown up. You could see the sky go red, so you knew you'd hit something. It was a great feeling. Then you'd go full speed out of there, at 40 knots. You'd do 35, 40 knots all the way back to Malta. You'd be back in Malta in the morning.

Lookout was a Lightning-class destroyer. They had twin 4.5-turrets, four of them, torpedo tubes and all the radar in the world. They call them a fleet destroyer [and] they could do about 42 knots. Very fast. They were a very modern destroyer and they used to go with the 'M's. The 'L's and the 'M's were the same type of ship. We were in a force called 'H' Force — there'd be three or four cruisers, and about eight destroyers all the time.

In July 1943 the invasion of Italy began when the British Eighth Army and the United States Seventh Army invaded Sicily. After fierce German resistance was overcome, plans were made to invade the mainland in early September by landing the United States Fifth Army in the Gulf of Salerno in order to seize Naples as a base for further operations. In preparation for the invasion of Sicily, the Allies sent bombers over from North Africa. One incident that Joseph remembers was when the aircraft were blown off course by the wind.

In those days they didn't have radar or directional beam finding or anything like that. They had to do it by sextant, if they could see the sun. They had one glimpse and found they were 20 miles off course. They corrected. The bombers were followed by American aircraft towing gliders full of paratroopers. They were coming in towards the southern part of Sicily, and the Jerries put up some ack ack. I saw the ack ack. I was standing on the port side of the bridge, and I saw all this flak going up, and then I saw the planes go out to sea again. Then they came in and just dropped the gliders. They pulled a lever and they dropped the planes and they buggered off. I saw the gliders and they went straight into the sea. A hundred miles off course. There were about twenty or thirty paratroopers in each glider. The paratroopers were drowned.

We arrived [back] there about a week later. They'd sunk and then they'd floated to the surface, and they were on the water — their bums were sticking up. They had full equipment on. We had to grab them by the neck, pull them out and open up their neck and we took off their identity tags — I call it a meat tag but they called it an identity tag. We had a bayonet each. They were all bloated, so we stuck the bayonet in and they sank with all their gear on. I did that for the best part of a day. I wasn't very pleased about it. After a while you got used to it. Not a very pleasant thing that, terrible.

In Salerno the Jerries had 8-inch guns up on the mountain where the British landed. On the first day we couldn't get near them because we only had 4.7 [inch guns]. We had to keep out of their range. I was standing there looking, and it was action stations. I was looking over the side and saw a big flat-bottomed barge. It looked like a gun. They called it a monitor, HMS *Erebus*, and it had a fifteen-inch gun the length of the barge. The next thing a big cloud of smoke came out — you know if you blow rings with a cigarette? Came out like that. She fired about five of these shells and cleared all of the guns out of the mountain. Everybody cheered.

We were there for three weeks at Salerno, up and down the coast, only about half a mile from the shore the whole time. The Yanks were further down the beach, and the British had the hills and Mount Vesuvius. We had to engage 88 tanks on the beach at Salerno. We'd been cruising along the beach. First of all the minesweepers went in, then the landing craft. We followed the landing craft into the beaches. We had been shelling there all night. Then about three days later we were all cruising along the beach and suddenly the skipper went around and came back head-on to the beach. The *Laforey*, that was the captain of our destroyers, went across our bow in front of us, and then these tanks on the beach shelled [him]. He got about four shells on board. One of the shells went right into the side of the ship and around B turret. B turret was a steel case and this shell hit it and glided around it. It never exploded, just did a complete curve round the turret then fell down to the deck. We were lucky, we didn't get hit there, but we did get bombed.

About a week, ten days, later we were cruising along. I was on the foredeck, the fo'c's'le, with just my underclothes on, lying in the sun getting sunburnt, and out of the mountain came these Me-109s. Straight out of the mountain, round Vesuvius and straight down. The fleet were there, and all the LCSs and LCTs and those sort of things. There were hundreds of bloody craft there. [The Me-109s] were machine-gunning along. I was lying there and looking at them. There was a Yankee destroyer about a mile or so away, she had all the guns loaded, and they must have had somebody in the control tower who just pushed the button and bang! It was gone. This bloody plane blew up in the air.

The size and intensity of the Mediterranean operations left a lasting impression on Joseph.

These landings in Sicily and Italy, they were tremendous. They reckoned they had about two thousand ships there. Well, you consider all that. There were the minesweepers first, and then there were the destroyers and sloops and frigates, and there were the cruisers. We were with the cruisers most of the time. You couldn't see the battleships, but they were there because you could hear their shells whistling above you. There'd be waves of planes. You'd see dots coming over and they'd be planes, groups of hundreds of them. A hundred there, a hundred there, a hundred there, a hundred there, and then behind that, there'd be another hundred. Right from the horizon. God, it was a wonderful sight to see.

We covered the landing at Anzio and were there for ack ack defence for a while, while our New Zealand troops were in Cassino, then we went back to Taranto through the Messina Straits, and up to the Adriatic. We had our Forward Observation Officer and we were shelling in front of the [ground forces]. We got as far as Rimini. We shelled there with the *Lively*. We were on our way back to Taranto when she ran into a mine. We pulled her out of the minefield and towed her right back to Taranto.

How long did that take?

About ten days. It's a long way. You wouldn't believe it but the Adriatic's a lot rougher than the other side of Italy. Sharp, choppy sort of a sea rather than a rolling sea.

It was after this that Joseph returned to New Zealand, aged 21, after four years in the navy.

I was in Taranto and I got called down [by one of] the officers and he said, 'You've been away a long time. Do you want to go home?' I said, 'Yes, please.' I waited until there was a suitable cargo ship, and I went down to Alexandria.

I came from Taranto down to Alexandria with about 108 New Zealand troops who'd been prisoners of war. They had been fighting with the partisans after Italy capitulated.

I went into the barracks in HMS *Sphinx* in Alexandria and got allocated to the cookhouse there. I was cleaning dishes and peeling spuds. It was good though, because right next door to HMS *Sphinx* was the New Zealand Army rest camp, Sidi Bishr. The guys who'd been prisoners of war were in Sidi Bishr. I was there for about six weeks in the cookhouse.

Joseph would take food from the cookhouse through to the army rest camp next door.

I'd go to these New Zealanders. They used to have a New Zealand issue of beer, Imperial Brown Bomber. It came from Auckland, I think. They got issued with two bottles each. I'd take the food through and they'd give me a bottle of beer.

Joseph then travelled by train to Port Said, where he spent a week or so before boarding a Polish merchant ship, the Kosciusko, *for the journey back to New Zealand. Here, too, he was joined by the New Zealand prisoners of war. He returned home in 1944 and resumed work for the railways in Wellington, where he completed an electrical apprenticeship. After leaving the railways he had his own business as an electrician for twenty years, before moving to Auckland and joining the Auckland Electric Power Board.*

Reflecting on his time in the navy, Joseph says that it was very pleasant to watch all of his ship's shells detonating along the coastline.

You didn't know what you were hitting, but you'd see all the shells go and somebody would tell you later that you'd hit something. Everybody in the ship had anxiety and a form of scaredness, but you got used to it after a while. You got used to the machine-gunning and the dive-bombing. You were sort of on edge. It's like: what do you do? You can't do anything. You weren't actually frightened. The only time I was frightened was when we were in the ammunition hole in the [*Walker*]. It was my first time out. I was just seventeen. You ducked your head and hoped you didn't get hit. Fortunately, our ship was the lucky one. Of the eight L-class destroyers, *Lookout* was the only one left at the end of the war.

'WE FELT IT WAS OUR DUTY'

JOSEPH BACOS, 42209, PRIVATE, DIVISIONAL ORDNANCE, 20 ARMOURED REGIMENT

Joseph Bacos, born in Dunedin on 3 January 1919, was the youngest of the five children of Habib and Saada Bacos, who had emigrated to New Zealand from Lebanon in the 1890s.

ALL I KNOW IS THE fare was £10 and they came on a German ship. How they found out about New Zealand we never bothered to ask, and I'm sorry I didn't. They didn't know each other [before they left Lebanon]; they met here.

My father couldn't find anything to suit his education. He became a traveller, a hawker, around Central Otago. He had a horse and cart, and he'd take drapery and go round the farms and towns. I went with him once with his horse and cart when I was about six or seven or eight. I can remember the various houses we went to — [in] Middlemarch, Sutton, Hyde, Central Otago. He'd say, 'I'll be back in June,' or something like that. He got to know a lot of people, and they would buy various items of drapery off him. We were fairly poor.

*Joseph's mother also worked as a hawker, selling
drapery and cosmetics, after her marriage.*

It was an unusual thing for a woman to do. She walked the
roads of Central Otago to help the family because my father
didn't bring in enough income, apparently. She had a big
perambulator with suitcases and boxes on it. A remarkable
thing, really. I used to go to the station and meet her every
time she came back. I think she liked the freedom.

We were subject to racism because we were different, we
were from the Middle East. We suffered quite a bit. We were a
bit sensitive about it. All that's disappeared now.

They could tell from our names and we were a bit foreign-
looking. They'd call us names — 'dagoes' — or make faces at
us. Generally treat us with disdain and sort of contempt: 'You
don't belong here.' And we felt that we didn't. I didn't feel I
really belonged, you know, until I put on the King's uniform
when I joined the army.

*Along with four of his friends from the Public Trust
Office, where he was working as a clerk, Joseph
enlisted in January 1940.*

I was 21. The war was only four months old but we reckoned
it was a just war on the part of Britain and we had loyalty to
Britain. Strangely enough — it might sound funny in this day
and age — but we felt it was our duty. The five of us used to
go and have a drink at the City Hotel and we decided, 'Yes,
we'll all join up.' That's how it happened.

One fellow wore glasses and was turned down. So he said

to the St John Ambulance man, 'Look, I had a bit of grit in my eye. It's affected my sight. Could I have another turn?' And the man said, 'Yes, OK.' He was busy. 'Wait over there.' In the meantime, my friend learnt the test. He came to work the next morning with it written on a piece of paper and gave it to me, because my eyesight would have been a bit suspect. I might have passed, but then again I might not have. I didn't want to fail.

There was also an extensive medical examination at the Drill Hall in Kensington, Dunedin.

They examined your lungs, your heart and your feet. If you had flat feet, you'd be turned down. Ridiculous. There were tons of jobs in the Middle East where you didn't have to move anywhere.

Joseph's father had died in April 1939, so he had only his mother to tell that he had enlisted.

She was a bit sad about it, but she understood. I was the only boy.

It was not until January 1941 that Joseph went into Trentham Camp, near Wellington.

We did just general infantry training for three months, and then I was assigned to Divisional Ordnance. It was the first time it had been created. They didn't have an ordnance prior to that. I didn't even know what it was.

They do repairs of trucks and instruments like binoculars, compasses, recovery of vehicles from the battlefield, things like that. We travelled with the division. There's Base Ordnance as well — same thing but it's in base. We were not a fighting unit, but we were a service unit.

Joseph left New Zealand on 6 April 1941 on the Nieuw Amsterdam *and travelled to the Middle East via Singapore, where he transferred to the* Aquitania. *He arrived at Port Tewfik in Egypt.*

The Arabs were being cursed about unloading, and there was commotion and people running back and forth. It was the East, my first impression of the East. It was quite different from what I'd experienced here.

Could you understand Arabic?
I could understand it a fair bit. Not completely, but a fair bit. I couldn't converse but the odd words I might know.

We went to Maadi Camp by truck and did infantry training. They had a canteen there, the NAAFI — Navy Army Air Force Institute — it was called. You could buy beer and they had chocolates, cigarettes, all sorts of things. They used to play housie. So we had a bit of entertainment, and we could get leave to go to Cairo. We'd go by train to Babeluk station in Cairo.

I remember the first day I went in — we arrived in a heatwave even for Egypt. It was 48 degrees. I had a bottle of Red Band beer and it made me tight for about three hours. It was the heat. I could hardly walk. On one bottle of beer!

What sorts of other things did you do in Cairo?

Went round the bazaars, what they called the Musqi. Little shops with trinkets, and this and that. They'd invite you in, give you a cup of coffee, hoping you'd buy something. You'd haggle over price.

I started off as assistant to the quartermaster. I had a 30-hundredweight truck and a driver. We used to go and get the rations every day and then pick up things for the unit we were in. After about six or seven months they put me into the orderly room as a clerk, to which I objected. I didn't want to be a clerk. I was a clerk in private life. After a while I applied for a transfer, but Japan had come into the war and they said, 'Oh, we can't let you go. We don't know when we're going to get reinforcements.' With Japan happening they didn't think they'd get any reinforcements, that they'd retain them in the Pacific. But I kept persisting and persisting, and they offered me promotion to orderly room sergeant. I didn't want that, so I turned that down. They finally let me out into 4 Brigade, which had been withdrawn after the first battle of Alamein to be converted into an armoured brigade because our infantry had been cut to pieces through lack of armoured support in the desert.

Joseph went with the New Zealand Division when it was sent to Lebanon in March 1942.

We were there in the Beqa'a Valley, and my unit was six miles from the village where my mother was born. It was quite an experience. I hitched a ride there. I spoke to somebody and he couldn't understand me much, so I spoke a bit in Arabic, what I could. He said, 'Come down here', and took me down to a woman. I started to talk to her. She spoke English very well. She happened to be the widow of my mother's brother. She went back from [New Zealand] to Lebanon. I wrote [my mother] a 22-page letter about it. They put on a big evening for me. I got some leave and stayed there and they put on a big evening with singing. I couldn't tell you — the food! I don't know how many courses they had, even though they were a poor community. They had chicken, they had roast meats, Lebanese–Arabic delicacies I knew, that we used to make out here. It was really great. And I took one or two of my friends along too. They enjoyed it as well.

Were there other men from Lebanese families who had joined up?
Yes, there were. None in my outfit, but there were in other outfits and they all made their way at some stage towards the towns and villages where their parents had come from.

> *Once Joseph had transferred from Divisional Ordnance, he had to undergo training as a tank gunner at the Middle East School of Gunnery at Abbassia Barracks in Cairo.*

We had Sherman tanks — American tanks. I was there for four weeks. We used to go out in the tanks, and have lectures, do firing [with] 75-millimetre shells. There were one or two accidents. The South Africans were in a tank and couldn't get the shell in, so they got a hammer to hammer it in and hit the percussion cap. It killed the lot of them.

It would be about August or September of 1942 that I was transferred to 4 Brigade. I passed as a gunner and I was then assigned to C Squadron of 20 [Armoured Regiment], which suited me down to the ground because that was a South Island regiment.

How many of you in a tank?
Five. A driver, spare driver at the front, and in the turret, the commander, the gunner (that was me) and a wireless operator. Three of us in the turret and two at the front, the driver on the left-hand side and the spare driver on the right-hand side.

In December 1943, Joseph went to Italy with 20 Armoured Regiment.

We struck winter in Italy. The snow, up in the mountains. It was cold. The coldest I've ever been in my life was at Orsogna.

Tell me about Orsogna. December 1943, was that?
Yes. C Squadron of 20 Regiment were supposed to support the Maori Battalion in the attack on Orsogna. It was a mountain town. Our tank had to go to the workshops because our gun was not recoiling properly, it was coming back very slowly. So we went to the workshops and I renewed acquaintances with my old comrades — the ordnance. We were there three days then went up to join the squadron and found out they'd gone into action that afternoon. Thirteen tanks had gone in and nine had been shot up and several of the boys were killed. That was the worst night I've ever experienced in my life. I wasn't afraid, I felt quite sad. Fellows I'd been talking to about a week

earlier. You know, stiff and dead. Never see their home country again. I don't think I slept that night.

The next day we went up to support the Maori Battalion — the attack failed. But that's when we got a direct hit — eleven o'clock at night — and it killed the spare driver, Shorty. A young boy of 22. It landed right in front of the turret. It was high explosive. Had it been armour-piercing we would have all been killed. He got shrapnel all over him and died the next morning. That was my first tank battle. Well, it wasn't a tank battle — my first time in action in a tank.

What was the countryside like? Was it suited for tanks?

Not really. Mountainous. Rivers, streams and forests. It wasn't tank country, not like the desert. The desert was ideal tank country, but no, Italy wasn't suited. The tanks were there to support the infantry, and we used to fire in support of the infantry on certain objectives. They'd ask us to fire some shells at so-and-so. But there were no tank battles as such. It was all mobility in the desert, but [in Italy] we'd be on a road and be firing in support of the infantry.

After Orsogna we went, I think, to Cassino. And that failed. We were supposed to be supporting the Maori Battalion again in their attack on the railway station. They captured the railway station, but they couldn't hold it because we couldn't get near enough to help them. It was the rubble. The whole town was a heap of rubble and we couldn't move.

We didn't drive the tanks out. We were there about three days and nights, then we were relieved. We walked out and the Canadians walked in and took over our tanks for three nights. To give us a bit of respite, I suppose.

And did you have to go back in again after that?

Yes, I think we did that twice according to my diaries. We were three nights there, we went out for three nights, came back again for three more nights, and by that time I think they'd aborted the Cassino attack. It had failed.

They couldn't even bury the dead. The stench of the rotting bodies is something I can still smell in my nostrils. The rats gorged themselves to the size of cats on the bodies.

Then we went up the Liri Valley supporting the 22 [Battalion] in an attack. That was when we nearly got killed because we were on the road, firing in support of the infantry. A British Don R came by and got shot in the shoulder. He was right in front of the tank, bleeding. His bike flew off to the side. We couldn't get out to rescue him, so what they did was mighty clever. They manoeuvred the tank over him [and] pulled him up through the escape hatch at the bottom. Bob Fraser, the spare driver, pulled him up. They then reversed the tank around the corner — it was a mountain road, not very wide — and when we got there they said, 'You boys had better have a breather. We'll send another tank forward.' So we got out and sat on the side of the road, just off the road on the grass. I remember Theo Dore, one of the sergeants, said, 'Listen fellas, you could be a bit exposed there. If I were you, I think I'd sit by the tank.' We got up languidly. We had no sooner reached the road when mortar bombs dropped right where we'd been sitting. So we owe our lives to him. We'd have been killed. That was a very close shave.

The Liri Valley was dangerous. It was here that Joseph also had a close shave with a sniper's bullet.

We were supporting 22 Battalion in a night attack. We left about nine o'clock, in pitch black, and at about eleven or twelve o'clock our tank came to a stop on a slope. It had shed a track. So, as dawn approached at about half past three, four o'clock, Nigel, our commander, said, 'We'd better move from here. We'll be a sitting duck.'

He got approval from Headquarters and we left the tank and walked off about a couple of hundred yards or so to a crossroads where there were houses. We stayed there for about two or three hours or more.

At half past eight, we thought we'd better go and get breakfast. Things had sort of died down, so I went down and took the wireless operator.

He got into the tank and as I got in a bullet hit the side of the turret [about six inches away]. I said, 'By jove, we'd better hang on here a while.' So we waited five minutes, and I put up my tin hat on the end of my Tommy gun as if I was coming out. Nothing happened, and I waited five more minutes and did it again. Nothing happened. I said to him, 'We can't stay here all day. We'd better just chance it.' The sniper must have moved on.

Joseph's unit then proceeded towards Florence.

I could see it in the distance. Some of the boys took French leave and took a truck and went in, but I couldn't. That's as far as I got — the last hill before Florence. I'd have loved to have seen Florence.

I had only one day in Rome. I went the first day leave was granted, had a look, and then a couple of weeks later I was due to go on ten days' leave on the Thursday. We went into action on the Wednesday, and that finished that.

We went into different towns. We were camped in a lot of the smaller towns like Atessa and Siena, Sora, Caserta. They were fairly big towns. We had a look through them.

Did you have much contact with the Italians?

Yes, quite a bit. We used to give sweets to the Italian children. They came clustering around. And salt, the salt! You got kissed on both cheeks. From the mothers — they kept their daughters away. (There were some nice-looking young women in Italy.) They'd say, 'Sale! Sale!' They must have been desperately short of salt. We got to know the Italians and we gave them quite a bit of food — cheese and bully beef.

We used to live in their houses as we progressed. They'd make one room available for us and we'd sleep, five of us, in this room. At night we'd sit in front of the fire with them. The boys had found some railway sleepers and they cut them up and piled them on and set the chimney on fire. The father of the house went up on the roof and he was screaming out, 'Acqua! Acqua!' So Bill went to the tank and got our extinguisher, and put it out. We had a fire from then on, but just a moderate one.

We used to talk to them in broken English and broken Italian. I remember one house — it was in Sora, I think. We were there about three nights, and a fourteen-year-old called Philomena, who was a friend of the daughter of the house, used to come up and sit, just sit, and not converse all that much. We used to take her home at ten o'clock. And we never laid a hand on her, of course. She was lovely.

Was there a black market in Italy?

Yes. Some of the boys would sell some of our food and that. I wouldn't allow them to take anything on our tank. The gunner is usually the second in command to the commander, and I wouldn't let them take any of it. We had a store of food there in case we were cut off anywhere. And I said, 'You're not taking any of this, whatsoever.' We'd have bully beef, canned sausages, a primus, margarine, cans of vegetables; enough to survive on for a few days if you were cut off somewhere.

Was there ever any trouble with the local Italians?

I remember once we were trying to pinch some potatoes that were growing, and a woman appeared with a pitchfork. She castigated us, so we didn't. Well, we couldn't — she had a pitchfork! They were short of food too, and it was pretty poor of us to go and pinch her potatoes. I think we finished up giving her some food, anyway. That was the only time.

Otherwise they treated us pretty well. They weren't antagonistic. We used to raid the wealthy people's houses, [especially] their cellars. They used to have lots of top-grade wines. I struck a small bottle of the most delicious drink I've ever had in my life. It slipped down like satin. The Maoris used to raid the cellars. At one of the cellars of a house of a wealthy person, they were drinking the wine and then dashing the glass into the fireplace. Freyberg came along and saw them. Gave them hell. I couldn't help laughing over that.

I felt guilty about one thing we did. George and I, we raided this house at Sora. It was empty, they had taken to the hills. We found a place that had been papered over, and he said, 'There's a room here.' So we got a pick and opened it and sure enough, there was a little room like a pantry. They had things stashed. They had a big box — we never opened that box — but he took some silk stockings and I took a silk bedspread, of all things. Stuck it in the tank. And I got half a dozen nice towels. I gave them away to the other boys. It was a rotten thing to do, really. I've always felt sorry about that. That's the only looting I did, and I felt guilty.

Was there much looting by other people?

Yes, there was a fair bit of looting. Mainly in the cellars, for the drink. The affluent people — we didn't hesitate about [raiding them] because we said to ourselves, they'll be Fascists, so blow them, we'll take what we can. But we didn't like to take it from the poor, the ordinary people.

I had been a year in the tanks and then I got hepatitis. I was called to the orderly room and [told], 'Your application for compassionate leave has been granted.' I said, 'I haven't applied.' 'Well,' they said, 'they must have applied in New Zealand,' which they had done, because my mother had had a stroke.

After treatment for hepatitis, Joseph was repatriated to New Zealand.

I went back to Cairo, to Maadi, and waited for a troopship, and I met up with one of my cobbers who was in the air force in Britain. He was going home on the same ship, the *Aranchi*. We went to Bombay and were there for two weeks. We got on an American ship called the *General John Pope*, and I arrived back here on New Year's Day 1945.

Two days before his 26th birthday, Joseph arrived in Wellington and travelled to Dunedin. His mother, although still sick when he returned, gradually recovered from her stroke.

What was it like coming back?
Well, it was sort of unreal somehow, as if it was a dream. Four years that had gone. They'd gone, and here we are. Quite unreal.

Joseph returned to the Public Trust but did not stay there long, as he did not want to be transferred from Dunedin because of his mother's health. He then worked in various administrative positions, retiring from a meat export company in Wellington. He married his wife, Grace, in 1951, and had three children. Joseph remembers his time in the army positively.

I thought we were well-treated; I thought we were well-led. We had some mighty good leaders and I think we carried out our duties pretty well, overall. In 20 Regiment, when I was in C Squadron, the one in command, Major Pat Barton, was an excellent fellow, excellent leader. His 2-i-c, Pat Abbott, was the same. They both survived all right. Even [during] the battle at Orsogna when Pat Barton got two tanks shot up under him, he got into another tank because he was the leader.

What made those two so good, do you think?
They had that something about them, that air of command and

efficiency, and they knew what they were doing. They didn't lack in spirit or courage. That's how they impressed me, the two of them. Excellent. And also the tank commanders I served under: Nigel Overton from Southland and another one, Owen Hughes — an excellent tank commander.

Do you think that the experiences that you had in the war affected you in terms of how you looked at the world and lived your life?

Definitely, definitely. I saw a bit of the world that I otherwise wouldn't have seen. I would never have spent three years around the Middle East. I would never have visited Lebanon, where my ancestors came from. I wouldn't probably have seen Rome or the byways and highways of Italy. It broadened one's outlook tremendously — coming from a little country in the South Pacific, and seeing the northern hemisphere and how other people lived and how lucky we are here.

The war didn't leave any scars on me. I never got scarred by the war. I never got depressed by the war.

'A PRETTY STICKY DO'

REG HERMANS, 27138, LIEUTENANT, 6 FIELD COMPANY

Reg Hermans was born in Ranginui, North Auckland, in August 1918. His father, Frank, was a railway and highways engineer, and Reg followed in his professional footsteps. The family moved to Wanganui and he attended Wanganui Technical College, and then Victoria University College while working for the Public Works Department. In June 1940 he enlisted with 13 Railway Construction Company, 2NZEF, and, after initial training in Hopuhopu camp, sailed for the Middle East with the Third Echelon in August that year. He served with the Railway Construction Company in the Western Desert before being commissioned in 1942 and posted to 6 Field Company, with whom he served in the North African campaign.

In May 1943 the New Zealand Division arrived back in Egypt following the surrender of the German forces in North Africa earlier that month.

IT WASN'T VERY LONG AFTER we'd arrived back in base that we heard that the people from the First, Second and Third

Echelons were going to be given the opportunity of going back home on furlough. I think, from memory, it was going to be a month at home in New Zealand before coming back to the Middle East. Ballots were held to pick people for what was called the Ruapehu Draft, which was the first draft to come home. People who were most eligible were married men and older men, people who'd been in Greece, Crete and the early campaigns and had survived. I remember Fred Hanson [the Commander Royal Engineers] telling me he wasn't putting my name forward because he couldn't afford to lose all his 'battle-hardened officers'. He had to have a nucleus of people who had been through a fair bit of action for when the reinforcements arrived over. And the Ninth and Tenth Reinforcements did arrive when we were in Maadi Camp before we went to Italy.

When word came that we were to go to Italy, the division marched from Cairo up to a place called Burg el-Arab, just out of Alexandria, which was our base before we went to Italy. We went by truck.

I went over in the advance party for the whole division. We set sail from Alexandria — we didn't know where we were going — and arrived in Taranto three or four days later. This was in September 1943.

Just out of Taranto we set up camp for the reception of the rest of the troops. It was two or three weeks before they came over. All the transport and heavy equipment came over independently again.

Once the company arrived we started doing more training, and it wasn't long before we got into action again. We started moving up in stages, repairing demolitions, demolished bridges and things like that, and putting in deviations.

The division was moving up the east side of Italy to engage with the Germans at the Sangro River.

There were several rivers to cross. The Jerries had demolished just about every bridge, so we were either replacing them with Bailey bridges or putting in deviations. A deviation is a temporary road to replace the bridge. We had to do this repair work to get the division forward. On one occasion my platoon was putting in a deviation, and I remember Brigadier Weir from the artillery came up. He said, 'You're wasting your time repairing this bit of road. You should be going across here', or something. I said, 'No fear. My instructions are that we've got to make it available for the division later this afternoon to come through.' In the middle of this argument, Tiny Freyberg arrived on the scene. 'What's the problem?' Steve Weir said, 'He's wasting his time, he should be going across here.' Tiny Freyberg turned to me and said, 'Do you reckon that you can get the division through here by four o'clock this afternoon?' I said, 'Yes. If I'm left to it, I'll do it.' He turned to Steve Weir and said, 'You mind your own business. He's my sapper officer. He knows what he's doing. Let him get on with it,' which I thought was quite amusing at the time — Steve Weir being told off in front of a two-pipper. And we did get the job finished and open in time for the division to go through.

Eventually we got forward, and the Germans had established the Gustav Line across Italy from the Adriatic coast to about Rome. The Sangro River was part of that defensive position, so that's what we had to break through. And so the battle of the Sangro developed. We were established in a static defensive position on the south side of the Sangro, and Jerry was on the other side with all his artillery, lobbing stuff down on top of us. We were doing the same, there was a lot of counter-artillery work going on. All the bridges on the Sangro had been blown, and 8 Field Company had the job of putting a Bailey bridge across a fairly wide part of the Sangro. I was given the job of putting across what we called an assault bridge — a folding boat bridge — further upstream on the 6 Brigade front.

These assault bridges — they wouldn't carry tanks or anything like that, but you'd get light artillery, machine guns and motorised vehicles across a folding boat bridge. I was given the job of locating a site for this bridge and then building it when zero hour came.

I had to do a reconnaissance to find a suitable site for this folding boat bridge. The idea was for us to find a site, then wade across the Sangro if it was shallow enough to get across, and do a reconnaissance on the other side to see whether we could get motorised vehicles over. The river, at that point, was a bit like the Rangitikei River here in New Zealand — a wide gravel river bed with shallow ribbon streams in the middle, with one particularly wide part — a couple of hundred feet wide. Jerry was just on the other side, so I took an infantry party with me from 24 Battalion. I think it was about a half a platoon, two sections.

Reg met the platoon commander on the riverbank.

We had a little conference and I said, 'I'll take an [infantry] runner with me and when we've decided, yes, this is a possible site, I'll send the runner back and you can come forward with your infantry types.' The idea was that half of them were going to stay on our side of the bank and provide covering fire if necessary for me and the other infantry people to go across and do a reconnaissance on the other side. Lieutenant 'Pig' Hunter and Sergeant Alan Begbie were with me on this reconnaissance.

We found what we thought might be a suitable site, and I sent the runner to bring his infantry blokes forward. They were about five or six hundred yards back, and we knew that there were minefields on this bank and that they were probably anti-personnel mines with tripwires, that sort of thing. Being used to working in minefields, we raised our feet up and down so that if we trod on a tripwire we pushed it down into the ground, we didn't drag it. It's like the front legs of a trotter, going up and down. I sent the runner back and said, 'We might have come through minefields, so bring your people forward exactly where we came through, preferably in single file.'

It was a miserable sort of a night, pretty dark. We were sitting there waiting for them to come forward and there was an almighty bang. A couple of minutes, there was another almighty bang. I said, 'Hell's teeth, they've got caught in the minefield. I'd better go back and see what's going on.' I retraced my steps, and I was met about halfway by their platoon commander. He said, 'I've lost half my platoon, either killed or wounded.' I said, 'Forget about it. You go back and look after your people, and I'll see what we can do.' I tried to wade across the river by myself but it was too deep, I nearly got washed off my feet, so I said, 'OK, we'll just have to estimate the width of the river to get an idea of how much of a folding boat bridge we need, and leave it at that.' Which we did.

The next day I went up to 24 Battalion and I wasn't

particularly popular, although it was no fault of mine. What happened was that instead of coming through single file, they spread out a bit and one of them tripped a tripwire, set off a mine, and they all went down. That was the lull that I heard. They'd lain down and then somebody must have said, 'Right, up we get and away we go,' and somebody must have had his rifle either on or under a tripwire and as they stood up, another one went off. I think they had about four or six killed.

Then zero hour was decided for the attack across the Sangro River, and we assembled at the start line. We had a couple of bulldozers with us, because it was a gravel riverbed. It was [the bulldozer operators'] job to prepare the approach to this folding boat bridge. Before zero hour, we tried to get down to the start line and had to go through a village that had very narrow streets. The leading bulldozer driver had the motor throttled right back; we were creeping forward, and he must have got the blade caught on a building somewhere and stalled the motor. We were getting pretty close to the river by this time. Those bulldozers have a little donkey engine — two-stroke motor, I think it was, made a heck of a noise — as the starter motor to start the diesel motor for the bulldozer. We didn't dare start that little motor because of the racket — it would have indicated to Jerry that something was going on. We had to sit there. We lost several hours, but eventually when zero hour went up we got going again.

The bulldozers were trying to make some sort of a wheel track across the river bed. One of them ran into a soft patch and got bogged. We brought the other one forward to try and drag this one out. It got bogged. It was a bit of a shambles, but anyhow, we eventually managed to get the bridging equipment up to the site and got cracking with building the folding boat bridge.

The intention was to do it all during the night and enable the light artillery, light machine gun and things like that to get across to support the infantry who had waded across the river. We'd just about got it finished — there was shot and shell flying around in all directions, of course — and were just putting in what was called the landing bay, and I was directing operations and there was an almighty bang behind me. I looked round and somebody's boot landed beside me. We'd got a direct hit from long-range artillery, right at the end of the bridge.

I went back across the bridge. Six of those carrying the last bit of equipment across, including Sergeant McIntosh, my platoon sergeant, had been killed instantly. This shell had landed right at the end of the bridge. There were dead and dying there, some of them in the river. It was a proper shambles. I took one look and said, 'We'll have to abandon.' There was no other way — I didn't have enough men to finish the job. I went back to the start line on the bank of the Sangro, and said, 'For goodness' sake, get as many stretchers as you can up to the bridge site to get the wounded out.' This was broad daylight and we were still getting hammered to hell with artillery and machine guns and Lord knows what. The infantry were up ahead of us — I couldn't make out what was going on, but we got the wounded out. Unfortunately, some of the men who hadn't been wounded got killed because they were standing up, helping the walking wounded to get out.

Number 2 Platoon was back, and I got as many of them to come and act as stretcher-bearers. We thought we'd just got the last wounded bloke out and then somebody sat up.

A sapper from the platoon, Ray MacFarlane, had stayed with me and I said, 'There's somebody wounded over there. We'll have to get him out.' We had no stretcher, so we set to and made a temporary stretcher using folding boat oars and rope, crisscrossed, and greatcoats. [We] put this bloke on the stretcher. I didn't check to see whether he was still alive or not. I assumed he was because he'd sat up. We carried him across the riverbed to a depression. Blasted Jerry was still chasing us. I heard a shell come over and said, 'Go down!' This shell landed only about six or eight feet ahead of us. By this time I was pretty exhausted and I said, 'We'll just have to leave him here.' He was in a sheltered place. 'We'll go out and see if we can get somebody else to pick him up and carry him out.' Well, it so happened that the poor bloke was dead when they got him out. He was Sapper David Hume.

It was a pretty sticky do, I can tell you that. I lost nine killed, and two died of wounds and another nine or ten were wounded in that one little episode. I lost about twenty out of a working party of 40. I had to abandon trying to get this bridge across, and I think one of the other platoons finished it that night. There was no way I could carry on and do it.

Reg was awarded an MC for his part in this incident.

We pressed on up to Castelfrentano and I was given the task of going with the infantry, again with 24 Battalion, in the first battle of Orsogna. My job was to repair any demolitions on the road up through Orsogna and to clear the road of mines; in other words, to make it possible for the tanks to come forward after the infantry. I was attached to Ted Aked's company, C Company, to go forward with them and get into Orsogna.

It was a wet, rainy, terrible night. I was tacked onto the back of this infantry company to go forward through the olive groves. I remember what sounded like bumble bees going through, and it was — you couldn't hear the machine guns, they were so far away — but it was the machine-gun bullets going through the olive trees above our heads. We were crawling through the long grass, of course.

In getting forward, I lost contact with the infantry. I wondered why we were taking so long to get through, and went forward. I couldn't find anybody so I said to my chaps, 'You stay here. I'll take a runner with me and go up on the road.' By this time it was dark. I went up and came across one or two Sherman tanks on the road. One of the tank commanders put his head out of the tank, and said, 'Who are you?' I said, 'I'm the sapper,' and he called me everything under the sun. He said, 'Look, there are mines across the road up there. We can't get forward because of these mines lying across the road.' Incidentally, when we were back in Maadi we had offered to give the armoured people a bit of instruction on how to lift mines in an emergency — 'Oh no, we know all about lifting mines.' Well heck, the first time they run across mines, they're calling for the engineers to come forward!

I went forward with this runner. There were three Teller mines lying across the road, on the surface. They weren't even buried. I always carried a long length of telephone wire, coiled up on my belt. I wasn't going to play around trying to disarm them or anything, so I put the telephone wire around and retreated back down the road about 50 yards and pulled on the wire until I was sure they hadn't been booby-trapped, then went back and picked them up and put them on the side of the road.

Not very far forward of that, I came across a demolition — the Germans had blown the whole road out. I checked this demolition for S-mines, and then sent a radio message back and said you'd better bring the dozers forward to make this demolition suitable for the tanks to get through. We didn't find mines of any sort, but it was right beside a haystack which was blazing furiously — probably deliberately lit by the Jerries to serve as an aiming mark for their artillery covering the demolition.

Off I went, further up the road, sweeping the road for mines. I called the tankies forward. 'Oh crikey, no,' they said. 'There's an anti-tank gun firing straight down the road.' I said, 'It's all right for you tankies. Here am I with my blokes, standing up sweeping the road for mines.' I didn't come across any that I can remember, but I saw some movement in the water table at the side of the road, and went over. It was the infantry. I said, 'What the heck are you doing here?' He said, 'We're taking shelter. Can't you hear that Spandau?' I said, 'Yes, I can hear a Spandau all right.' He said, 'We can't get any further forward.' I said, 'Who's in charge, who's your commander?' He said, 'Our platoon commander — he's right forward.'

By this time I'd told my chaps to get down. It wasn't a particularly safe place to be. I crawled forward and found the platoon commander and we had a bit of a discussion. I said, 'What's the problem?' He replied, 'We can't shift this blasted Spandau. We've thrown grenades and all sorts of things at him. We can't get forward.'

I said, 'No place for sappers to be. What are you going to do?' He said, 'All we can do is go back and talk to our company commander about it.' So off we went back to this pink house and there was Ted Aked, the company commander. It was cold and wet as hell and they'd set up the RAP, Regimental Aid Post, in this house to look after any wounded. By this time I think Ted Aked was the only company commander left in the infantry. They'd taken a fair sort of a battering.

One tank squadron was behind us waiting to come forward, so we said, there's only one thing to do, and that's to get the tanks to put down a stonk on this blessed Spandau, and get rid of him that way. We got hold of the squadron commander. He reckoned he couldn't get forward with his tanks, despite the fact that we'd cleared the demolition. He reckoned there was an anti-tank gun firing down the road, and if they went forward the first tank would get knocked out and block their way, and the contours of the country were such that the tanks couldn't get forward through the olive groves. They decided to stay where they were, a few hundred yards behind us, and put down this stonk.

When they opened up with the 75-millimetres that they had on the Sherman tanks at that stage, all hell broke loose, as you can imagine. Talk about dust. The whole house shook and the dust was coming down from the ceiling. Everything was blacked out. Prior to that we'd had a bit of light from either hurricane lamps or candles, but now it was all dark.

There was a double door on the bottom storey of this house with a bolt on it. One of the infantry came in just before the stonk started; he had a walking wounded with him and took him through to the back where they'd set up the Regimental

Aid Post, and he left the door open. Ted Aked and I were sitting by the fire, and I stood up and closed the door. He said, 'Don't bolt the door. There's some more walking wounded coming in behind me.' By this time the stonk had started. I stood up, opened the door, unbolted it, and there was an almighty bang just outside the door.

I went flying. My leg was lying over to one side. I thought it had been blown off. This blessed shell, or whatever it was, landed just outside the door and caught me right up my left-hand side. There was no sign of Ted Aked, but when I called out to him he came over and tidied me up.

For me the war was over. I'd been pretty badly wounded. Then they had to get me out somehow or other. They got a stretcher. We had my scout car there with us, and I had to give instructions on how to fit a stretcher across the back of a White scout car. Back I trundled. I wasn't particularly comfortable. We had been issued with morphine capsules and I did have two or three in my battledress jacket pocket, but I'd used a couple of them at the Sangro. I knew I still had one there, so I told them they'd better give me an injection of morphine because I wasn't very comfortable. They gave me this injection, trundled me back to where the ambulances had been parked up — three or four miles back — and put me in this ambulance. I was the only one in the ambulance. I didn't move, didn't move. I don't know, I must have been bleeding like a stuck pig at the time, and I must have been fading in and out of consciousness. I can't remember a heck of a lot, but I do remember the door of the ambulance opening again and somebody else on a stretcher being put in, and somebody said, 'Are you still here?' And did he get stuck into the ambulance driver. I can remember the ambulance driver saying, 'My instructions are that I'm not to go back until I've got a full ambulance.' Somebody must have given him the message. Incidentally, the ambulance had chains — it was so muddy, it had chains on all four wheels. Anyhow, he got the message that he had to take us back.

The net result of this was, I was wounded at about ten o'clock at night and it was breaking daylight when we got to the ADS about six miles away. It had taken just about all night to get me back there. My femur was fractured. I was caught between my knee and my navel. I wasn't aware of the internal [injuries], I was more concerned about my leg.

They put the stretcher on a couple of trestles and the MO came over and examined me. I can remember him saying, 'Hello, how are you? How are you feeling?' and I said, 'Awful. Do you think you'll be able to save my leg?' That was all I was worried about. 'Save your leg?' he said. 'That's the least of your worries.' And that was the last I remember for a couple of days.

I can't remember how long I was in the ADS, but I remember being transferred by ambulance again, with tubes and all sorts of things around me and my leg in a Thomas splint, back to the Casualty Clearing Station, which was several miles further back. I didn't realise how badly wounded I was. Probably nobody who's wounded knows how bad they are. At the CCS I did have an internal operation. To keep me alive, I suppose. I remember coming out of the anaesthetic and the sister was cleaning my fingernails. She said, 'What dirty fingernails you've got.' That was hardly surprising considering what I'd been through!

In due course I got onto a hospital train and went back to Bari hospital, 3 New Zealand General Hospital. I arrived there at about midnight. We were all laid out on the stretchers in a big foyer awaiting, I suppose, an initial examination and then to be sent off to the various wards. Eventually I went up into the officers' ward, and talk about cramped. It was a room that would normally hold two hospital beds, and there were five of us in it. By this time it was one or two o'clock in the morning, and they came and said, 'Would you like a cup of Bournvita and some nice hot buttered toast?' 'Would I what!' So they brought this along to me, and it was real buttered toast. I thought I was back in heaven.

Within pretty short order, I was taken down to the theatre and when I came back I was in a Hip-Spica plaster. All I could move was my head and my arms, I was in plaster from my chest down to my toes, except for my right leg, which was in plaster down to my knee. I was just like a log. In this plaster there were holes in appropriate places to attend to my needs, but I couldn't do anything for myself.

They'd put me in plaster to put tension on my leg. It was a nice clean break but the muscles had contracted and it had telescoped by about an inch. They'd taken me down to theatre to try to stretch my leg, put a Steinman's pin through and plastered it up to try and hold the leg. It was the only way they could put any sort of tension on it.

Reg had two or three operations while at Bari.

They had the stretcher at the end of the bed, lifted me up and put me on the stretcher and took me feet first out through the door. With my leg, even in plaster, it'd give me hell when they were lifting me onto the stretcher. But anyhow, I survived.

After about a week they decided to change my plaster because I'd developed pressure sores under the plaster and they'd suppurated. They put me in a new plaster. I was a lot more comfortable because they put more padding in. I was in that plaster, I suppose, for about four or six weeks.

There were no such things as counsellors, for heaven's sake. The chaplain used to come around and have a chat. [The surgeon] would come and do his rounds close to midnight, and he'd be there again at six o'clock the next morning doing his rounds again. How the dickens they kept going I don't know, but they did a marvellous job, no question about that.

Reg spent Christmas 1943 in Bari hospital and was visited by some fellow officers on Christmas Eve.

By this time I was so weak I could only talk in a whisper, but I do remember them sitting around my bed drinking some sort of alcohol, possibly whisky.

Come the end of January they came and said, 'You're going on a hospital ship.' I thought I was going home, but no, it was a Tommy hospital ship going to Egypt. I embarked at Taranto. I suspect it was to clear Bari hospital out for future casualties from battles that the division was going to be involved in.

It took about four days to go from Taranto across to Alexandria. I must have got bronchitis or something, because I remember I had a blessed oxygen mask on for most of the trip. I didn't enjoy that trip. I wasn't in my plaster, but I had all my other tubes and things around me because of the internal injuries.

Reg was then taken by train to 2 New Zealand
General Hospital at Helwan.

It must have been some time in February that I was transferred
from Bari over to Helwan hospital — and towards the end
of March, at long last they came along and said, 'There's a
hospital ship coming in and you're going on it back to New
Zealand.'

We had to go by train from Helwan, which was out of
Cairo, not far from Maadi, down to Suez to be put on a hospital
ship at Tewfik, to come back to New Zealand. Under normal
circumstances that would have been a three- or four-hour trip
on the hospital train, but we got a couple of hours out of
Cairo and a sandstorm hit and covered all the railway tracks,
so we were stuck out in the desert in this hospital train for at
least a day, possibly even a couple of nights. And stink. We
had no facilities and there were chaps there with abdominal
colostomies, amputated limbs, in plaster, and you can just
imagine the smell in the train in about 100 degrees Fahrenheit.
How the poor nurses coped, I don't know.

Eventually we got down to Tewfik and got on board the
hospital ship, *Maunganui*. I was a stretcher case. The very
small hospital beds — 'cots' I think you'd call them — were
pivoted at each end so that when the ship rolled, you didn't
get rolled out of bed. The only scenery I saw was either the sea
or the sky through the glass porthole, depending upon when
the ship rolled.

The liner Maunganui *was converted in 1941 into*
a hospital ship with a theatre, surgical theatre,

> *and accommodation for the medical and nursing*
> *staff.*

I still had open wounds being attended to. I don't know how many shell splinters went through me, but they were moving so fast that they didn't stop, so there was no shrapnel left in my wound. It had all gone clean through because I was pretty close to the shell when it exploded, so it was travelling at pretty high speed. I've got some pretty massive scars. One of my wounds was in my groin and it developed gas gangrene. [The doctor] said, 'We'll soon fix that.' He daubed it with methylated spirits. Well! Sting! There were bars on the bed behind my head. I reckon I very nearly bent the bars. The agony of the methylated spirits on that raw wound. Oh hell! It cured it all right.

There was plenty to do to fill in the time on the voyage back to New Zealand. I read books, they had a library, and there was canned music [which was played in] a request session. They'd come round to the beds with a typewritten sheet of all the records they had. I think it was on for an hour in the morning and an hour in the afternoon. We were allowed to choose ten requests to come over the air. I'd participated in a bit of Gilbert and Sullivan when I was at school, you know, *Mikado* and *Pirates of Penzance*, so if there was any Gilbert and Sullivan, I'd request that. There were a few modern things too. 'Accentuate the Positive' was a popular tune. We used to have that a bit.

We had a physiotherapist and occupational therapist on the ship with us as well. The walking wounded used to come around and have a chat to you. You weren't lying there bored to bitter sobs.

We called in to Colombo for revictualling and refuelling on the way home and some of the walking wounded managed a few hours ashore but, of course, the stretcher cases were bedbound. At Fremantle, however, some of the local ladies came on board with baskets of fresh fruit, and I remember one giving me a freshly picked apple, which I very much appreciated.

It was 29 April 1944 when we arrived back in Wellington. Stretchers were put on the ground on the wharf. It was raining and a couple of dear old ladies were standing with their umbrellas over us, trying to keep us warm, and tears were running down their faces. I said to Doug, 'Hell's teeth, we must look a lot worse than we think we are.'

We were put into an ambulance and taken up to Wellington Hospital. Wards 21 and 22. Ward 21 was downstairs and Ward 22 upstairs. Home in a New Zealand hospital again.

I was put in a hospital bed, with my leg strung up in all directions and a few tubes here and there. My file was within arm's reach, so I got it. The first entry, much to my amusement, was 'A well-nourished young man'. I thought, gee, if Mum saw that, wouldn't she be pleased? I think I was only about seven and a half stone when I arrived back. When I eventually got onto my feet, the best part of twelve months later, I managed to get onto the scales and I was nine stone one — a big difference from the thirteen and a half stone that I weighed when I was wounded.

They came and assessed me and X-rayed me and transferred me from the military ward up to the urological ward. I found out later that one of the reasons was that both kidneys were chockablock with stones and I was barely surviving. I lost count of the number of operations I had in Wellington Hospital.

I must have been on penicillin for at least nine months — in fact, until the wound in my leg healed up. I was pretty fortunate as it had only come into use fairly recently before I was wounded. Osteomyelitis was diagnosed in my leg soon after I was wounded — hence the penicillin.

Reg was discharged from hospital in March 1946, nearly two and a half years after being wounded. He returned to the Public Works Department. When he retired in 1978 he was the District Commissioner of Works in Hamilton. After his retirement he was a member of the Planning Tribunal, now known as the Environment Court, until 1986. He reflects on his wartime activities:

As far as I was concerned, all I was interested in was getting an RSA badge when I got home. That was my objective: to get home in one piece. I didn't manage it, but that was all I had in mind when I was over there.

'A PENNY TO GO TO THE WAR'

Douglas PARK, Lieutenant Commander (A), Fleet Air Arm

Doug Park was born in Dunedin in December 1918.
He attended Musselburgh School and Otago Boys'
High School before beginning work as 'the boy' at
the National Insurance Company in January 1935.
The worsening international situation in the late
1930s made Doug feel he should join the Territorials,
which he did at the beginning of 1938. The Otago
Regiment was a machine-gun battalion. Shortly
after the outbreak of war he was transferred by his
company to Invercargill, and joined the Southland
Regiment.

I DIDN'T ENLIST RIGHT AWAY, for what reasons I can't remember. I had a brother about four years younger than me. He had intended to go into the air force on a short service commission, which was what a number of New Zealanders did in the late 1930s. It was partly because he had wanted to fly that I thought that I would prefer to be in the air force, so early in 1940 I enlisted in the air force, hoping to get in as a pilot.

Conscription wasn't in, but there was talk of it. It was decided that NCOs would be called up for two or three months' training so I, with the others in the Southland Regiment, came up to Addington Raceway in Christchurch, and we were in camp there for two or three months.

In April 1940, while he was in camp at Addington Raceway, Doug heard that he had been accepted for the air force but would not start his training until January 1941. He returned to work in Invercargill briefly before being transferred by his company to Wellington.

And had that not happened I don't think I would have got into the Fleet Air Arm. Out of the blue, I got a letter from the navy in Wellington, saying we know you've enlisted in the air force and are due to go into Levin at the end of January 1941, but have you ever thought of transferring to the Fleet Air Arm, because you can sail for England almost right away. Well, this attracted me. I had to have another medical, but apart from that there was no interview, no nothing.

Doug was accepted and sailed for the United Kingdom on the Akaroa in January 1941, having become engaged to Doreen Stuart before he left.

My father came up with me to Wellington, and my fiancée and her mother. I reported down to the RNVR — New Zealand then didn't have its own navy, it was a division of the Royal Navy — and was told we would sail the following day. I went back home and had a night there, and said farewell in the morning and reported again to the headquarters. We were told that we were not sailing now till the next day, so we went back and had a second goodbye the next morning, and reported finally to headquarters. I got on board the ship just at lunchtime. I remember quite well sitting down at the table, about quarter to one. I looked out the porthole and saw that the wharf was moving, so we left our lunch and went up on top to see the end of Wellington.

We did a big sort of loop down the south of the Pacific and came part of the way up the South American coast. It was probably about a day from there up to Panama. There was a Japanese naval vessel in, tied up not too far away from us, and we were doing great yahoos to them. We didn't necessarily think that Japan was going to come into the war at that stage, but we just gave them the one, two a few times and they shouted back at us and that was it.

When we arrived in the UK it was blooming awful. We'd been treated pretty well on the ship — we were in civilian clothes, we had four of us to a table, we had a waiter to serve us food, had two to a cabin, we had sheets. And then we hit England.

We arrived off Cardiff in Wales. It's a tidal harbour there and we had to wait for the tide. We could see the shore, we could see cars — it was daylight — and then we heard an air-raid siren. We looked up and an aircraft went over, quite high up, a single aircraft. We recognised it from the air recognition exercises that we'd done. It didn't do anything, except it went round in a circle and flew away.

We landed at Cardiff and had to go down to Portsmouth harbour to a place called Gosport, opposite Portsmouth city. We thought all the world would be out to meet us. Well, when we got ashore we had quite a job to find out what to do, but somehow we got on a train to Portsmouth. By the time we finally arrived in Portsmouth late that night, ten or eleven o'clock, we were fairly hungry. We expected the mayor of Portsmouth to be there with food for us, but when we got there, again there was no one there that knew anything about us. We eventually raised the local barracks at Portsmouth and they sent a truck up to the station for our luggage. We had to walk. We were told that we were going to spend the night at the naval barracks in Pompey [Portsmouth] and go across the harbour the next day.

The first thing that we grizzled about when we got to the barracks was that we were hungry, because we hadn't eaten for hours. That wasn't very well received, because it meant that they had to get the cooks up out of their bunks and cook up some soup for us. We had no bedding, so we had to get the sailor in charge of the bedding store up out of his bunk, and go and draw hammocks. None of us had ever slung a hammock before. We were shown into a barrack room where there were hundreds of sailors asleep or half-asleep in their hammocks. And you can imagine what it was like with 35 of us arriving, having no idea what the routine was in the Navy, not knowing how to sling a hammock. 'Shut up, you bloody New Zealanders,' and all this coming from the other guys. We were shouting out to them. It was about half past one in the morning when there was finally a degree of quietness. We were dog-tired, and it seemed like no time at all before wakey wakey went and at six o'clock we had to turn out and get our feet on the deck.

There was a parade at nine o'clock. It was a big barracks;

there must have been several thousand sailors on parade there. We were still in our civvy clothes, and the 35 of us were right at the front. When the commanding officer came along with his flag lieutenant and one or two others — I could quite easily hear because he was only a couple of metres away from me — he turned round to his flag lieutenant and said, 'What is this?' The flag lieutenant said, 'They're New Zealanders.' He turned his head the other way and marched on.

The parade was over. We had taken more than we should have by way of suitcases and impedimenta, and we eventually got a truck that took it all down to the ferry — we walked — but the crying out thing was that the fare across the harbour was a penny. We didn't have a travel warrant, so each of us had to pay a penny to go to the war in the Portsmouth ferry.

We got to the other side, and as we went through the gateway of HMS *St Vincent* — it was an old naval barracks going back about 50 or more years — as soon as we got through the gateway, there were other sailors there, New Zealanders, and they said, 'You silly buggers. You're mad. You should not have come. You should have stayed at home. This place is dreadful.' Which was a wonderful greeting. Of course, we in our turn went down a month later to the next lot and did the same to them.

We lived there for something like three months, because the flying schools, through bad weather and one thing and another, couldn't take us, and so we were there rather longer than we had intended to be.

We were kitted out and shown where the air-raid shelter was, and [told] that any time that there was a double red, which meant enemy aircraft overhead or in the very near vicinity, we had to go into the air-raid shelter. It was a dugout trench in the ground. It was cold and dank and unpleasant. We had an air-raid warning more than once every night, so we thought it was routine, and then one night somebody put his head out of the shelter during an air raid and dropped dead because a bit of shrapnel had taken his head off. So we realised that the commonsense thing was to keep underground and not poke your head out during an air raid.

Sometimes we were ashore when an air raid would start. This one night, I must tell you, it was the most hellish night, I think, that I've ever had. I was across in Portsmouth with some others at a cinema. I had a feeling that there was going to be trouble that night. I came out of the cinema about half past seven. The other boys stayed there and I said, 'No, I'm going home.' I went from the cinema down to get the ferry, when the guns and searchlights started up. Knowing a bit more about it now than I did then, it was a puny raid compared with what happened later. There was only something like 400 tons of bombs dropped over a period of four or five hours. That was absolute peanuts compared with what happened later, but it seemed to be an incessant rain of bombs. I got out of the cinema to go down to the harbour, and it got too hot to walk in the street at all. I passed another shore station called HMS *Vernon*, and I got in there and was shown to the air-raid shelter.

The bombs seemed to be coming down all the time. It wasn't really like that, looking back on it, it just seemed as if it was every minute or so. Anyway the thing slackened off after a couple of hours, and I was still determined to get across to home, so I got out of *Vernon*, went down a few hundred metres towards the wharf and it started up again. I got into an air-raid shelter down there, and some others came in and told me that the air-raid shelter at *Vernon* had just been hit by a string of bombs and that there were a lot of casualties up there. We eventually got down to the wharf. There was no ferry at that time — it was two or three o'clock in the morning by then — but there were some naval launches running across to the other side and I got in and went over to another naval barracks — not where I should have been — and stayed there for a couple of hours. I had breakfast there and went home in the morning. I found out when I got home that they'd had a hell of a night where I was. Nothing was actually hit at the place, but there were big oil tanks not very far away and some of those tanks had been hit with incendiaries and they'd gone up and that made the thing look awful. I was in many other [raids] worse than that, but that was my first one and it sticks out in my mind. I can remember the date, it was 10 March 1941.

Doug eventually went to train at Elmdon airfield, near Birmingham.

They had lovely little aeroplanes, Tiger Moths, and very pleasant RAF instructors. There was still a vague possibility of an invasion. I don't mean a mighty big invasion, but there was the possibility of paratroopers coming in, and so little bomb racks were put on the Tiger Moths. They were going to put eleven-and-a-half-pound bombs on these bomb racks to counter the invasion. We were to be sort of armed guards for the aerodrome and, you wouldn't believe it, but we were issued with pikes. A pike is two or three metres tall with a big heavy metal spear on the end. We used to do pike drill.

Did you like flying? Was it easy for you to learn?

I thought I was going to love it. I found after a couple of hours or so that I was airsick. This worried me a lot and the more I worried about it, the more I didn't feel like flying because I knew I was going to feel sick. I couldn't take things in if I was feeling like that. So I went to the doctor, and found it wasn't unusual. There were one or two others in the same way, but I hated to be in that lot. The doctor said, 'If you take glucose half an hour before you go up, that sometimes helps.' For a few days I took glucose before I flew and almost overnight, I didn't feel airsick. So that was good.

And then came the great day — you'd only done about seven or eight hours flying — but the great day when you go solo. My instructor said, 'You're ready to go. You can go tomorrow.' Tomorrow turned out to be a bad day for weather and I didn't fly. The next day I went solo — on 27 July 1941, my fiancée's 21st birthday.

I was airsick later on in the Mediterranean. Some of the guys were really sick, but that was a combination of rough seas and then taking off and flying in rough weather. The motion was quite different, but if you tended to be seasick, you could be seasick and airsick within a couple of hours of one another, so that wasn't very pleasant. But that was rare.

Doug spent six weeks at Elmdon and then continued his training in Canada on Harvards, under the Empire Air Training Scheme. He returned to the United Kingdom at the end of January 1942 and was sent to the West Country to learn navigation before going to a naval air station at Crail in Scotland, where he learnt to fly naval aircraft, Swordfish and Albacores. He practised dive-bombing, formation flying and dropping bombs and torpedoes. He was then posted to Arbroath to learn deck landing.

For three weeks or so we did nothing else but learn how to deck land. I think it was a minimum of 120 day deck landings on the runway at Arbroath, and 20 night ones. If you couldn't do that, you failed. Most of us got through that and we went over and did our deck landings on the *Argus* in the Clyde. You had eight to do. If you did what you'd been told to do, then you should be OK. We knew that you could feel the pull of the arrestor wire on your aircraft after you landed, but we didn't have landing wires on the aerodrome, so the first time that we ever had experience of an arrestor wire was on the carrier. It was a little bit strange because you were pulled up fairly suddenly.

Not everybody had the opportunity of getting to a carrier-borne squadron because there weren't enough carriers for the number of aircrew. A number of operations for the Fleet Air Arm were done from aerodromes. At that time there were five fleet carriers. We went flying for a little while ferrying repaired aircraft, just generally waiting round to get posted to an operational squadron. Then came the day when I and a couple of others were posted to a squadron in Gibraltar.

We went out in a carrier called the *Argus*. It was an extremely rough voyage. Apart from the day before I got into Lyttelton at the end of the war, coming through Cook Strait, it was the roughest sea that I'd ever been in, going across the Bay of Biscay. We didn't have an opportunity to do any flying on the way out to Gibraltar until the last day. About 300 miles or so west of Gibraltar out in the Atlantic, we flew ashore. I'd never been there before, and it was fun flying over the water and seeing the Rock and landing there, on the single strip.

When we got to Gibraltar, nobody seemed to know anything about us. We reported to somebody who was in the squadron we'd been sent out to relieve and were told we weren't wanted. They didn't know anything about us at all, and we could go and get lost because they were not prepared to have us.

So we were there for a week or so, wondering what was going to happen to us. Nobody could tell us, or [they] didn't know. We had Christmas there in the mess, and we did some anti-submarine patrols over the Straits, just for want of something to do, but then, early in January 1943, the *Formidable*, one of the fleet carriers, came in. It was part of the force that had gone out for the North African landings in November. There was a torpedo-bomber squadron on board, 820 Squadron, and they wanted two spare pilots and a spare observer. We were just going to be there to fill in somebody's shoes if they went missing. We decided amongst ourselves — we cut cards, aces high, for the two pilots; the navigators could make their own choice. I got an ace, and the only other New Zealander in our group got a king.

We went down to the carrier, went on board and reported to the Commander Flying, and he had a look at our log books to see what we'd done. He knew we were very junior and obviously if he didn't want us or didn't like us, we'd have been told, but no, it was fine. We could join 820.

The squadron had been together for about a year, they all knew one another. There was a New Zealand observer in the squadron, but not a New Zealand pilot. There were some other New Zealand pilots in the fighter squadrons on board. We had a Seafire squadron and a couple of Martlet squadrons and the New Zealanders generally were pretty popular, as I found when I joined.

> HMS Formidable *had a crew of around 1900 on board, of whom between 80 and 90 were aircrew.*

I had done no night deck landings on a carrier but the rest of the squadron had, so I did my nights at sea off Gib, and from then on, though a new boy, I was really accepted. The deck had small outline lights, and those and the batsman's signal lights were the only lights in the total blackness. It was essential to be on the ball for night landings on the carrier.

What sort of action were you involved in on Formidable*?*
We were part of Force 'H'. [We had] two British battleships. I can't remember just exactly at that time whether it was *Warspite* and *Valiant*, because we had them for quite a bit of the time that I was in the Med, but we also had *Nelson* and *Rodney* at one stage, and the *King George V* and the *Howe* — but I think that was later on, for the attacks in Italy. So there were a couple of battleships, and there were us, and six or eight cruisers and about fifteen destroyers. It was quite a good force.

The big reason for staying there, after the North African landings, was to be a counter for the Italian navy. The chance of it coming out wasn't very great because it had got such a hiding from the Royal Navy in years gone by, but the Brits had to have something there in case they did. They were largely based in Taranto in Italy, which was a couple of days steaming along, so for some months at the beginning of 1943, we would go to sea from Gibraltar for three or four days, call in at Oran, maybe [spend] a couple of days there, then go to sea for three or four days towards and beyond Algiers, but not ever as far as Taranto. We'd get so far along there, and then we'd turn round and come back again. We were patrolling and doing day and night anti-submarine patrols with four depth charges.

We did a few anti-submarine patrols from shore bases. One of the beauties of being in a carrier was that we had this home at sea, but we could also be flown to aerodromes ashore and operate from there, both by day and night.

The carrier had many powerful anti-aircraft guns, but its only real operation was to be a floating aerodrome for the aircrew. We swamped the mess a bit. There were ship's officers there as well, but with all the aircrew — nearly all the pilots and observers being officers — there were lots of fairly junior officers in the wardroom. We were not encouraged to drink. The bar was there, and it was a big temptation seeing the ship's officers having a couple of snorts before dinner. We never knew, if we were at sea, if we were going to have to fly or not, so it was stupid to have any spirits. It was as cheap as peanuts. Gin, I think, was a penny, and the dearest thing was a penny-halfpenny a time. You could go through quite a lot of booze at prices like that. If we knew we were going to be in harbour then we would have a bit more hilarity.

There were four squadrons on board. We were the biggest because we had observers, whereas the fighter boys had only pilots. Although we were all mates together, each squadron had its part of the wardroom where it habitually gathered. We didn't relate too much, squadron to squadron. Now and again somebody from another squadron would come over and join you, but by and large we kept together. There was no great hilarity. The ship's company had been with flying people for some time, they were very used to it. They put up with all our drunken songs. We had some dreadful songs. We used to sleep a fair bit. We would play cards, mostly poker.

What was good on the carrier was deck hockey. It was a great game. You got a chuck like ice hockey, and a stick like ice hockey, and a net at two ends, and you could do that on the flight deck. Mostly the ratings played, because they were even more bored stiff than we were. Now and again, when we were ashore at an aerodrome, the ratings would have a soccer ball and they'd kick that round, but there wasn't any particular sport. There was no gym on board, there was no facility really for anything like that except you had the wonderful flight deck where you could have this hockey game.

Most of us were sub-lieutenants. At 25, if you had done everything right, you got your second stripe, which was lieutenant.

Tell me about the invasion of Italy.

Well, eventually came the time when the North African thing was over. The Germans had surrendered and North Africa was clear of them, so obviously the next step was what Churchill called 'the soft underbelly of Europe', and that meant putting an army ashore in Italy, first of all Sicily.

So the troops were all gathered for that. We had been along as far as Alexandria before the invasion of Sicily, partly because we had a bit of engine trouble. We also needed the ship's bottom scraped and there was a dry dock in Alexandria, so we went along there for a couple of days to have that done. The fleet stayed in the Algiers area while we and a couple of destroyers went along to Egypt. The New Zealanders on board the carrier were allowed a couple of days leave to go down to Maadi, but when we got down there we found they were away on manoeuvres so we did not see them. One of the guys with me had a brother in the Pay Corps and he was still at Maadi, so we met up with him.

We came back to join the rest of the fleet in Malta for the invasion of Sicily. Again, we were not going to be taking a major part in the actual invasion. We were placed as a fleet in the Bay of Taranto, in case the Italian fleet came out, which it didn't. All the landing craft for the invasion of Sicily — and the Americans and the gliders and the paratroops — they were all slightly over to the west of where we were. There were one or two unfortunate incidents we weren't involved in. Some American aircraft got lost and flew over part of the fleet and got fired at. I think there were some casualties, but that didn't happen where we were, we just heard about it later on.

Whenever the fleet was at sea, we were on anti-submarine patrol — two aircraft were up for three hours, day and night. Then we found that the troops had got ashore all right in Sicily. We still stayed up there towards Taranto. We didn't go into Taranto. We were largely doing anti-submarine patrols for the fleet in case there was an Itie sub there. Sicily ultimately was taken, and that was that.

We were back in the Malta area for a short time before Salerno. The Germans were retreating slowly up Italy, but it was thought that if we could put a force in part of the way up Italy, that would hurry up the ones that were lower down, so there was a big invasion plan for there. From the navy point of view, it was to be supported by a fairly big fleet. There were five smaller aircraft carriers than us, and the *Formy* [*Formidable*] and the *Indomitable*, but unfortunately the night before the invasion of Sicily, the *Indom* had a German torpedo put up its backside and that was the end of that. It went off to the US of A and for a little while we were the only big carrier there, but just before Salerno we were joined by the *Illustrious*. We were to give protection to the invading army at Salerno. We weren't operating over Salerno. The fighter planes, largely Seafires, from the five smaller carriers were to do that until an air base had been secured in the area, when the air force would have then come in.

We heard that there was a German dive-bomber squadron coming down from the Rome area. The night before Salerno there was a fairly big fleet there, and army transports with soldiers and infantry on board. Our schoolmaster on the carrier could speak German and was listening in to the German radio and relaying what he was hearing to us through the ship's loudspeaker system. Knowing that there was a German dive-bomber squadron there, he somehow got on to their wavelength and heard the German leader of the squadron saying they were ready to attack. 'And here's the bloody fleet. Oh my God, it's the fleet, it's not the army, it's the navy.' There was a heck of a lot of anti-aircraft stuff going up at this time, so I wasn't at all surprised that he was surprised at what he'd run into. I don't know whether they dropped any bombs. There was so much stuff splashing in the water, you couldn't tell what was what and it was night-time anyway. But a tremendous barrage of stuff went up and they must have turned round and gone home, because they thought they were attacking the army invasion fleet but unfortunately it was the Mediterranean fleet. They used to send reconnaissance aircraft out to see what was going on, but the Brits by this time had fairly well [got] command of the skies, so that there wasn't a lot of intrusion by enemy aircraft.

The night before Salerno the Ities had surrendered. During the morning, I can remember flying on anti-submarine patrol in a fairly big fleet — I think we had six battleships at that stage, plus a considerable number of cruisers and destroyers — it was a lovely looking fleet. An Italian submarine was coming down between the fleet and the shore, on the surface, and we noticed that there were some Italian sailors on the submarine, stripped off and lying back sunbathing. They were all right because they'd surrendered the night before and were doing what they'd been told to do. That was to go down to Malta and surrender properly to the Brits down there. And the fact that there was a dirty great war going on in their homeland was beside the point. They'd surrendered. They were not part of it. They were having a good time.

A couple of days later we went back to Malta. By this time quite a few of the bigger vessels of the Italian fleet were lined up outside the main harbour at Valetta, and just in case there was any funny business, our fleet went to action stations when we got within a few miles of Valetta harbour. I wasn't flying that day, but we had torpedo aircraft up just in case there was any funny business from the Ities as we came in.

There was a wonderful welcome going into Valetta harbour. The cliffs lining the entrance were crowded with Maltese. They were extremely pleased to see the British fleet come back into Malta, because they'd been through hell with air raids from planes based in Italy and Sicily, and now all that was gone.

Within a couple of months Doug had returned to Gibraltar, and at the end of October 1943 he was back in the United Kingdom. The squadron was to convert to Fairey Barracudas with a view to being posted to the Pacific, and Doug spent some time training on the new aircraft. Instead of going to the Pacific, however, he was posted to 767 Squadron at Easthaven airfield as a deck-landing instructor. He was promoted to commanding officer of the squadron, a job he was told would not be for longer than six months. Six months and one day later, the second atomic bomb was exploded in Japan. After a few weeks' leave in London, Doug set sail for New Zealand on the Stratheden *and arrived home at Labour Weekend 1945 on the* Andes.

When we got to Ashburton we had a wonderful reception from the Women's Division of the Farmers' Union, who turned on an enormous spread of morning tea. We got to Timaru, where the similar Division there turned on a magnificent lunch, which we had trouble in eating because we'd had such a big morning tea so soon beforehand. We finished that and got back on the train and [went] down to Oamaru, where again there was an enormous afternoon tea prepared for us by the Women's Division. Then we went to Palmerston — it was late in the afternoon by this time — where there was an even more enormous afternoon tea arranged for us there by the Women's Division. Of course, we could hardly eat a thing. And often, when I come past Palmerston, I think of that day when those women went to so much trouble and we couldn't do the decent thing and enjoy their afternoon tea.

Doug married his fiancée, Doreen, three weeks after he got back to Dunedin. He returned to work at the National Insurance Company and was transferred to London as manager not long after his wedding. The couple lived there for eleven-and-a-half years and then Doug was transferred to the firm's Sydney office. After five years in Australia, he returned to the Dunedin head office as marine underwriter for the company, and retired at the end of 1979.

Do you think your experiences during the war affected the way you lived your life after the war?
Well, yes, I think they probably did. I had more confidence. So much had happened to me — some bad, but so many good things had happened to me during the war that I felt confident that whatever job I was given I would be able to manage.

I feel content that I served and survived.

Joseph Pedersen
JOSEPH PEDERSEN
COLLECTION

Joseph Bacos
JOSEPH BACOS
COLLECTION

Reg Hermans
REG HERMANS
COLLECTION

Douglas Park
DOUGLAS PARK
COLLECTION

Newton Wickham
NEWTON WICKHAM
COLLECTION

Patricia Hamilton
LIZ CATHERALL
COLLECTION

Gordon Johnston
GORDON JOHNSTON
COLLECTION

Reginald Minter
REGINALD MINTER
COLLECTION

Rae Familton
RAE FAMILTON
COLLECTION

Jack Somerville
PHILIP SOMERVILLE
COLLECTION

Isobelle Wright
ISOBELLE WRIGHT
COLLECTION

Tautini Glover
TAUTINI GLOVER
COLLECTION

Gordon Slatter
MARIE SLATTER
COLLECTION

Members of the 'Div' stop for a cup of tea near the Sangro River, November 1943.
ALEXANDER TURNBULL LIBRARY, WAR HISTORY COLLECTION, DA-04638

A New Zealand soldier with a puppy he has rescued from the ruins of Sesto Imolese, April 1945.
ALEXANDER TURNBULL LIBRARY, WAR HISTORY COLLECTION, DA-09213

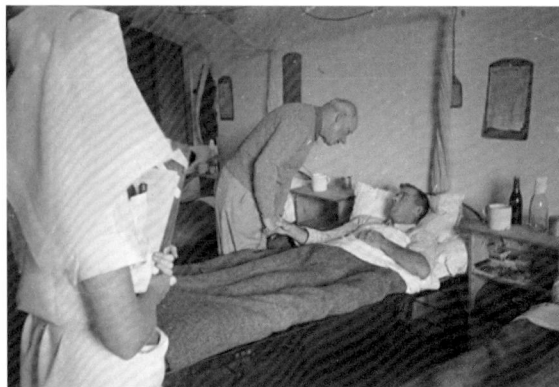

Prime Minister Peter Fraser talks to a patient at 2 New Zealand General Hospital, Caserta, June 1944.
ALEXANDER TURNBULL LIBRARY, WAR HISTORY COLLECTION, DA-06020

Lieutenant General Bernard Freyberg (second from right, front row) enjoys a performance of the Kiwi Concert Party in Italy with his troops.
ALEXANDER TURNBULL LIBRARY, WAR HISTORY COLLECTION, DA-05772

A New Zealand tank crew during the fighting near Florence, August 1944.
ALEXANDER TURNBULL LIBRARY, WAR HISTORY COLLECTION, DA-06481

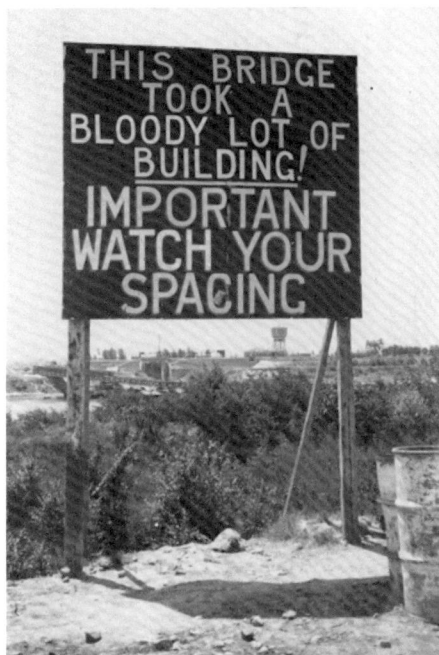

A sign erected by South African engineers with which New Zealand sappers would have heartily concurred.
ALEXANDER TURNBULL LIBRARY, WAR HISTORY COLLECTION, DA-03744

Maori soldiers with a civilian car — the fruit of their entrepreneurial skill.
ALEXANDER TURNBULL LIBRARY, WAR HISTORY COLLECTION, DA-07686

Joseph Pedersen's ship, HMS *Lookout*, in port at Malta, 1942.
JOSEPH PEDERSEN COLLECTION

New Zealand tanks near Orsogna, 1944. ALEXANDER TURNBULL LIBRARY, WAR HISTORY COLLECTION, DA-14621

An Italian child greets Joseph Bacos and his tank crew.
JOSEPH BACOS COLLECTION

Kiwi soldiers in Pesaro, one of many small Italian towns devastated during the war.
ALEXANDER TURNBULL LIBRARY, WAR HISTORY COLLECTION, DA-06642

Snow covers a New Zealand tank near Orsogna on New Year's Day, 1944.
ALEXANDER TURNBULL LIBRARY, WAR HISTORY COLLECTION, DA-14619

Melting snow and thick mud — typical conditions during January 1944.
ALEXANDER TURNBULL LIBRARY, WAR HISTORY COLLECTION, DA-05020

Winching a gun into a new position on the Sangro River front.
ALEXANDER TURNBULL LIBRARY, WAR HISTORY COLLECTION, DA-04694

Vehicles cross the Po on a folding boat bridge built by New Zealand engineers.
ALEXANDER TURNBULL LIBRARY, WAR HISTORY COLLECTION, DA-03299

Doug Park at La Senia airport in Oran, Algeria, December 1942.
DOUGLAS PARK COLLECTION

New Zealand engineers move forward in the wake of the retreating Germans, June 1944.
ALEXANDER TURNBULL LIBRARY, WAR HISTORY COLLECTION, DA-05984

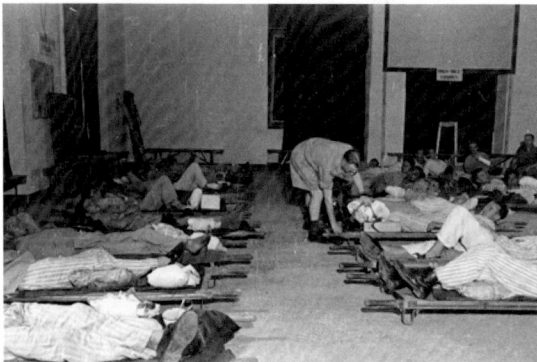

Wounded men on stretchers in the foyer, 3 New Zealand General Hospital, Bari.
ALEXANDER TURNBULL LIBRARY, WAR HISTORY COLLECTION, DA-08439

An Albacore lands on the deck of HMS *Formidable*, 1943. Douglas Park collection

Men wait for treatment outside 1 New Zealand Mobile Dental Unit, Italy, 1944.
Alexander Turnbull Library, War History Collection, DA-05650

Newton Wickham in the back of his mobile dental surgery, with Mount Cairo, near Cassino, in the background.
NEWTON WICKHAM COLLECTION

Pat Hamilton (right) on the tea counter at the New Zealand Forces Club, Cairo.
LIZ CATHERALL COLLECTION

Pat Hamilton on a picnic with New Zealand troops, Bari.
LIZ CATHERALL COLLECTION

Men in the lounge of the New Zealand Forces Club, Cairo.
ALEXANDER TURNBULL LIBRARY, WAR HISTORY COLLECTION, DA-01299

A tractor and gun of the New Zealand artillery cross a newly finished bridge.
Alexander Turnbull Library, War History Collection, DA-04698

Concert at the New Zealand Forces Club, Hotel Badiglione, Florence.
Alexander Turnbull Library, War History Collection, DA-07669

A New Zealand tank surrounded by crowds in Trieste.
Alexander Turnbull Library, War History Collection, DA-08396

Luciana and Gordon Johnston on the day they became engaged, 14 July 1945.
Gordon Johnston collection

A New Zealand Divisional Signaller makes contact by telephone in Faenza, December 1944.
ALEXANDER TURNBULL LIBRARY, WAR HISTORY COLLECTION, DA-07969

New Zealand ambulances wait near Cassino.
ALEXANDER TURNBULL LIBRARY, WAR HISTORY COLLECTION, DA-11792

A New Zealand truck destroyed near San Michele, August 1944.
ALEXANDER TURNBULL LIBRARY, WAR HISTORY COLLECTION, DA-06514

Christmas Day in Faenza. ALEXANDER TURNBULL LIBRARY, WAR HISTORY COLLECTION, DA-07993

A New Zealander in the ruins of Cassino signals to a tank in another part of the town.
ALEXANDER TURNBULL LIBRARY, WAR HISTORY COLLECTION, DA-05711

New Zealand tanks wait to cross the Adige River, March 1945.
ALEXANDER TURNBULL LIBRARY, WAR HISTORY COLLECTION, DA-03291

Empty charge cases at Cassino show the intensity of shellfire, March 1944.
ALEXANDER TURNBULL LIBRARY, WAR HISTORY COLLECTION, DA-05456

Resting Kiwi soldiers read captured German periodicals, Atina, May 1944.
ALEXANDER TURNBULL LIBRARY, WAR HISTORY COLLECTION, DA-05927

This Regimental Aid Post truck is typical of those used by 2NZEF in Italy.
ALEXANDER TURNBULL LIBRARY, WAR HISTORY COLLECTION, DA-05637

Thanksgiving service at Perugia. ALEXANDER TURNBULL LIBRARY, WAR HISTORY COLLECTION, DA-10946

A statue of the Virgin Mary stands undamaged in the ruins of Cassino. ALEXANDER TURNBULL LIBRARY, WAR HISTORY COLLECTION, DA-03750

Italian children at a party organised by 21 Battalion, March 1945. ALEXANDER TURNBULL LIBRARY, WAR HISTORY COLLECTION, DA-09035

Isobelle and Lawrence Wright on their wedding day, 2 April 1945.
ISOBELLE WRIGHT COLLECTION

A group of 28 (Maori) Battalion soldiers in Sora, June 1944.
ALEXANDER TURNBULL LIBRARY, WAR HISTORY COLLECTION, DA-06147

Maori Battalion soldiers prepare their dinner.
ALEXANDER TURNBULL LIBRARY, WAR HISTORY COLLECTION, DA-05124

One of the many piano accordions in the New Zealand Division.
ALEXANDER TURNBULL LIBRARY, WAR HISTORY COLLECTION, DA-10049

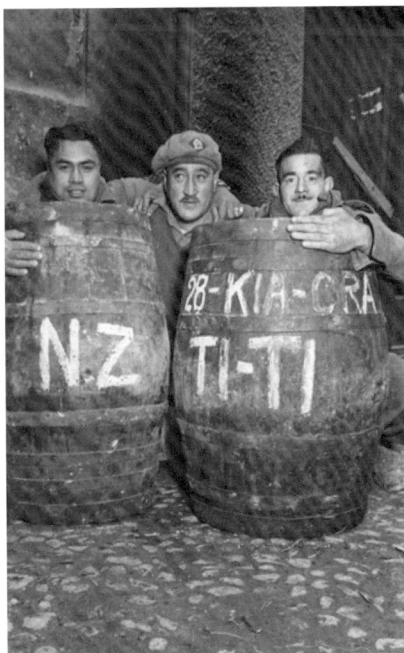

Troops from the Maori Battalion with barrels of muttonbirds (titi).
ALEXANDER TURNBULL LIBRARY, WAR HISTORY COLLECTION, DA-07989

Infantrymen of the New Zealand Division waiting to be taken forward to the front line, October 1944.
ALEXANDER TURNBULL LIBRARY, WAR HISTORY COLLECTION, DA-07712

During the feast to celebrate the return of the Maori Battalion, January 1946.
ALEXANDER TURNBULL LIBRARY, JOHN PASCOE COLLECTION, PAColl-0783, F-16631/4-

New Zealand soldiers and Italian children run a piggyback race in Muccia, March 1945.
ALEXANDER TURNBULL LIBRARY, WAR HISTORY COLLECTION, DA-09034

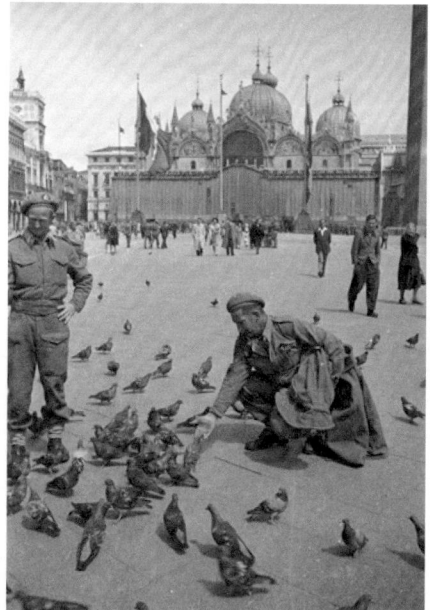

Feeding the pigeons in St Mark's Square, Venice, the day after the city was liberated by New Zealand troops.
ALEXANDER TURNBULL LIBRARY, WAR HISTORY COLLECTION, DA-09297

'A DIFFERENT TYPE OF WARFARE'

NEWTON WICKHAM, 19306, MAJOR, DENTAL CORPS

Newton Wickham, the younger of two children, was born in Stratford in May 1917. His parents both came from farming backgrounds, but the family moved to Auckland while Newton was quite young, and he attended Mount Albert Grammar School. After leaving school in 1934 he trained as a dentist at Otago University, graduating in May 1939. While in Dunedin he joined the Otago University Medical Corps and won a university 'blue' for hockey. After graduating he moved to Wellington.

I HAD A CONTRACT WITH Wellington Hospital as what was called a 'dental intern'. I lived with the house surgeons and I did emergency patients coming in throughout the night, and worked in the dental clinic during the day. I had a contract for a year, and that took me from May 1939 to May 1940.

My predecessor left and joined the army — the war started, so he joined up. When I was dental intern there, a nurse down in Casualty gave me the white feather. I went on duty and she put the white feather on me. That's some special sort of honour that not many people have had! I just walked away.

Newton clearly recalls hearing that war had been declared in September 1939.

I remember I was with a house surgeon, Alistair Loan, who was a very staunch Baptist, when it was announced on the radio. He said, 'Let us pray,' and we just knelt down beside the bed and prayed. That poor man went off up into China and he was captured and had a terrible time. What lay ahead for us, that night? The world suddenly began to change.

Because of his contract with Wellington Hospital, Newton did not join up immediately.

It gave me additional experience, especially in maxillofacial work and fractured jaws, which I had to deal with overseas. I got to be able to do anaesthetics, which stood me in really good stead later on.

Did you want to join up?

Yes, too right. It wasn't because of the adventure of it. We were quite plain when we went away: we want to get this job done and get back home. Fix this job up and get it done. But underneath there was a sense of adventure, and of the great unknown out there.

When I joined up, I was proud to be in uniform. I had to join the Dental Corps; I didn't have to go and kill other guys. I didn't have too much danger. I had rank but, above all, I was doing something I believed in. I was helping, really helping the war effort.

*Newton joined the Dental Corps with the rank of
lieutenant, and was a major when demobilised. He
was in a mobilisation camp in New Zealand for
fifteen months before being sent overseas.*

We worked long hours, late at night, because a group would
be going overseas and we had to get them finished before
they left. They were dentally fit before they left. That means
no cavities in the teeth. We did fillings — I remember doing
65 fillings in a day. Although the emphasis was on keeping
natural teeth, we still had to do mass extractions. We did
mass production of dentures. Fifty per cent of soldiers had
full dentures. Half of them. Young men, the cream of our
nation — full dentures. Incredible. So the New Zealand Dental
Corps had to be geared towards maintenance of dentures. That
meant we had to have dental services right up near the front,
because if a fellow loses his denture he's a casualty. He has to
go right back to base. This happened to the Tommies — the
fellow would be out of the line for weeks and weeks — but
not with us.

The soldiers' teeth were checked again when they got
overseas. And then when they got to their unit there was a
mobile dental unit which did routine treatment, and they'd be
called up for that. If they were wounded and went to hospital,
there was a dental officer there. Everywhere they were cornered
by dental officers, so it was extremely well organised.

*Newton left New Zealand for the Middle East in
September 1941 on board the* Aquitania.

That was a huge ship — 45,000 tons. I remember when we went down to the wharf to board the thing, all you could see was this great side of metal alongside you.

I was in Burnham, so I came up to Auckland on final leave. We lived out at Clevedon at the time. I think of my mother at the train. It must have been pretty grim for her. She said goodbye to her son. Here I was going off. The women had it tough.

After spending some time at Maadi Camp, Newton was posted to the mobile dental unit out in the field.

It was a unit of twelve officers, and each officer had an orderly, a dental mechanic and a little truck and a driver. The unit operated in a tent, a huge tent called the Big Top. The boys hated it, because it was a heck of a thing to put up. That was the mobile dental unit which did routine work, but then we had three Field Ambulances which did the casualty work and also a certain amount of routine work, each with a dental officer. That was further forward than the mobile dental unit — as far forward as you'll get. The dental officer with the Field Ambulance had a variety of work. I did my dental work and when there was a battle on, I looked after battle casualties. Fellows, they got brewed up in tanks and I'd peel their skin off. When tanks brewed up the men suffered terrible burns. Tanks get hit and they go on fire. The poor beggars are trapped inside.

I gave anaesthetics. At one stage in the desert I worked for 36 hours, and I thought, Oh God, can't you stop it just for a few minutes. Blood. And the dust. The cook brought me mugs of Ovaltine to keep me going.

When we got back after the North African campaign and before we went to Italy, I had a big unit made up. And blow me down, when it was being transported over to Italy, it was dropped from a great height on the wharf, killed two Ities and broke up my truck. I had to go down and salvage the dental equipment.

I was the only one who had a truck like that. In the base camp at Maadi we had proper buildings and a proper set-up like a dental hospital, but when we went out into the field we operated in a tent. It was a bit special because it had a higher ridge pole. We needed a bit more light to come in. But then I had an idea. My transport was a big truck, a three-tonner truck, so I devised the system of building the back part of it like a dental surgery. The front part carried what were called 'medical comforts'. It carried extras, tins of peaches and things. And the brandy — medicinal, of course — was in that part. I had to look after that.

The front part was partitioned off and had access from the front. I had the back part. I had a dental chair there, and I got them to fit some cupboards. I gradually assembled my own group of good instruments and I'd take them with me. It didn't take too much time to dismantle it and get on the way again. The dental mechanic was on the side. He worked in what we called the penthouse, which came down as a lean-to tent on the side. When we moved, that tent went up on the top. The role of the dental mechanic was to make dentures.

When the battles were being fought, did you then have to deal with the casualties?
Yes, they were brought down. You see we were a bit behind

where the fighting was. The Field Ambulance had an ADS — Advanced Dressing Station — and then the Main Dressing Station, which was where I was stationed. It was a unit of about 250 men. The ADS would send the patients [back]. They would collect them and they'd be put in the ambulances and brought back. So we were the first ones to treat them.

As they were brought in on the stretchers the medical officer's job, in the reception tent, was to go round and decide [what needed doing]. Some wounded, you just had to let die. Awful decisions had to be made.

Any emergency sort of work would be done at the MDS. They'd get an initial sort of treatment, then they went back to a Casualty Clearing Station which served the whole group. And from there, they'd go back to the general hospital, right back.

When the casualties came in and they had, perhaps, a shattered jaw, what could you actually do for them?
Immobilisation is the best thing. All the bits are loose and the jaws fall back, so the person can't breathe properly. What I'd do, I'd wire the teeth together. I had to do this by torchlight. My orderly couldn't bear to see all the blood and goo, and he'd look away and the torch would go. Some of them took me three hours to sort out all the little bits. And the bits of shrapnel. But I didn't get very many of them, because if a fellow gets hit around the head it's usually lights out for him.

It was dry, arid desert as far as you could see. I've got a mental picture now: as we were moving forward, the trucks would travel a hundred yards apart. This way and this way [in every direction]. As far as you could see were trucks, each with a little puff of dust behind it. All moving relentlessly forward. It was quite a picture.

And what about when you were in Italy?

It was so different. We changed to a different type of warfare. In the desert it was fast-moving, in Italy it was mud and rain and snow and cold, and short distances between battles. It was a bit different in our Field Ambulance. We had shorter distances to evacuate, so we didn't have to do as much work on the patients in the field ambulance, because they were going to get back to a CCS or hospital pretty quickly. So it was different.

And we used to sometimes live in the houses, take over the houses. There was a little girl, I think she was aged seven, Marie Concordia, and she'd stand and throw snowballs at me as I went past. This was at a place called Atessa. A lot of the fellows met up with girls, and we had one funny story. We moved from Sora to another place, and some of the girls who'd made friends with the [troops] moved as well. You'd see them up there. And someone referred to them as our Sora links, because we had soya links which were sort of sausages. Awful things in tins. Every unit had its wit.

Cassino is in my memory. That's where General Kippenberger was wounded. He trod on a little mine that didn't have any metal in so it couldn't be detected. A shoe mine, it was called. He walked on this and blew both his feet — didn't blow them right off but they were pretty loose. So he was brought into our Field Ambulance. You can imagine the panic. The General! We had a custom of placing a patient on a stretcher on two trestles with a big black kerosene heater underneath. One of the orderlies must have left this heater turned up too high and too long and it burnt Kip's backside. We were all sworn to secrecy, mustn't say a word about this. So away he goes, he's evacuated. Goodbye Kip. The next time I meet him, I'm in England with the returned POWs, looking after the repats. He was in charge of the whole thing. One night, I went up to him and said, 'Sir, remember when you were wounded at Cassino? Did your legs give you much pain as you were being evacuated?' He said, 'No, Wickham, but for some reason I developed very bad bed sores.' He never really knew why.

At Cassino it was snow everywhere. The thing that affected me most was trying to do dentistry with chilblains. My feet got wet and I was standing in mud. One day I tried to do it with boards beside the chair because I couldn't get the truck into position. There was no electric light in the truck. We had electric light, but not for that sort of thing. We had an electric generator. You'd go into camp and it'd be connected up so you'd have lights around the place, but not enough for that sort of thing. In order to get the light to do your work you had to be exposed and, yes, the rain would come in. We put a sheet over the patient.

Cassino really was grim.

When you were in Italy, where did you sleep?

In Italy I had that truck, and the sergeant (the dental mechanic) slept in the penthouse. I shared a tent with another officer. It was really quite comfortable. I had a fold-up stretcher and a bedroll, or valise. You had this canvas thing and the blankets went inside, and when you were sleeping, two flaps of canvas came over the top of you and one down over your head so you wouldn't get wet, to any extent. All this and the blankets were rolled up. The bedding was done that way. It was reasonably comfortable. When sleeping in a slit trench we would make a hip hole and shoulder hole to be more comfortable. And the batman came in with a cup of tea in the morning. I didn't use a batman much. We never had sheets, of course. You just slept in the blankets. And now and then they got washed.

It was cold. At Cassino we used a brazier. You put charcoal in it. They bought charcoal from the Ities. A big heap would come down and we'd all help ourselves. The brazier was just a little tin with a wire loop on it and you could swing it round. You put a bit of paper in it and then charcoal, and then you'd swing it round and round so the charcoal got glowing. Then you could put that in your tent. But it produced carbon monoxide and guys would put it in their little bivvy tent, and they'd pass out. This happened quite often, actually. In Cassino, when we took over from the Americans, the guys in the evening would be swirling these around everywhere and the Americans didn't like that. They took a few shots at them.

After the hostilities ceased in Italy, Newton went to England to work in the prisoner of war repatriation unit that the New Zealand authorities had set up in southern England, under the command of Major General Howard Kippenberger.

Life was unreal there. I realised that the prisoners were going to be scared of the real world because they'd been in a protected society. No women. And they were going to find it tough. It made me more sympathetic towards them. I went over from Italy on VE Day to take over a dental section. They had to be cared for dentally before they were sent home. Part of it was orientating them back into society. A lot of care was taken about this. And our unit, their duty was to have a party every Thursday night and invite local girls. We used to ring the local 'wrennery': 'Send down half a dozen Wrens.' Actually, all they were interested in was the food that we put on, I think.

After his time at the prisoner of war repatriation unit, Newton was given the opportunity to further his dental studies. He did postgraduate work at Toronto University Dental School before returning to New Zealand in 1946. In 1948 he married Keitha Kenrick, who had also served overseas, as a VAD, and the couple had two daughters. Newton practised as a periodontist — the first in New Zealand — specialising in periodontics and preventive dentistry, until his retirement in 1976. After the war he served in the Territorial Force. He was the commanding officer of 1 Mobile Dental Unit for three years, and then Colonel Commandant of the Dental Corps for eight years. He boasts that his unit, 1 Mobile Dental, once captured two SAS personnel! Reflecting on his war service he feels that he was a bit fortunate.

I got a certain amount of adventure, but not too much. I got an MID, yes, for being a good boy, generally.

'WORKING VERY HARD'

Patricia HAMILTON, 48403, Tui (Women's War Service Auxiliary)

Pat Hamilton (née Sherriff) was born on 16 March 1915 in the Rangitikei town of Marton. Her father, Humphrey, died in 1925 and although times were hard, Pat, her two sisters and mother, Ellen, managed on the small amount of money they had. Pat began work at the Marton Sash Door & Timber Company in 1929 as an office junior. She spent many happy years there till she went overseas as a Tui in 1941.

Can you remember when the war started?

The real impact of it didn't hit us until after war was declared and, as time went on, our boys started leaving the town. In the early stages of the war a WWSA group formed, Women's War Service Auxiliary, and they formed small committees in each town in New Zealand. Girls in each town put their names down — each group saying they would do canteen work, or Red Cross work, or drive trucks. It wasn't official, it was just a record of women who could be called on if they were needed.

We didn't take it very seriously. Olive Barton, a friend of mine, and I joined the canteen because I couldn't drive. We gave the odd cup of tea to the Home Guard, which was quite a jovial social afternoon.

Late 1939 it started to hit us, because our friends were enrolling in the air force and the army, and going away. At this stage Ohakea had a big air force base training camp, and when they held dances the girls used to go down in buses to spend an evening dancing at Ohakea. We met quite a few of the boys who were training as observers and pilots and gunners, and they became friends. In their off-duty time we used to invite them up to our home and take them for picnics [or] down to the river for swimming. They finally went off to Canada and then on to England, and many of them were killed.

What happened next?

I was living a very desolate life in Marton because my friend had gone overseas as a pilot. Life was very quiet and very worrying and very grim. I was surprised one day to receive a telephone call from Mrs Wallace, who was the secretary of the local committee of the WWSA. She said that the main group in Wellington had received a cable from General Freyberg saying that the New Zealand Forces Club in Cairo was established but it was a desolate place, with the suffragis staffing the counters, and he wondered if girls from New Zealand could be sent over to make the club a more homelike place for the troops on leave.

Olive and I had a ring from the WWSA group in Marton saying we had been chosen to go to Wellington to be interviewed by the WWSA. We travelled to Wellington and met dozens and dozens of girls who had gathered from all over New Zealand. We were feeling pretty depressed by the time we came home. The interview was OK. We didn't really understand what we would do. There wasn't much coordination between Cairo and here.

Do you remember any of the questions you were asked at the interview?

No. I don't remember the interview, but I know that I dressed very carefully in flat shoes and a plain grey flannel skirt and a grey sweater with a tailored white tussore silk blouse collar, and we behaved very carefully. We met girls who had come from everywhere. Some of them were so lovely and so confident. I remember one girl who swept in with silver fox furs draped over her shoulder and a very, very confident voice.

Why did you want to be chosen?

I had no idea how long it would be before we came home, and I knew that I would be leaving my mother whom I adored, but I was 25, and she was so enthusiastic for me if I had the chance to go to see some of the world and to take part in this war, that any reservations I had about leaving her were swept away. And, of course, I was wildly excited. It was a wonderful opportunity to escape the confines of a small country town, a very miserable little town in the war.

We received a telephone call one day telling us that we had both been chosen to go overseas, and this was the beginning of a new adventure for me.

Did you have any idea of what you would be going to Cairo to do?

No, I wasn't sure at all. I thought that maybe I would be doing clerical work in Alexandria. When we went down to Wellington we were taken into the 2NZEF and we became members of the 2NZEF. We were put on a par with the soldiers for pay and things that we had to be issued with. We were issued with clothing. We had two officers — two older women — and two sergeants and the rest of us were privates, but we never used the rank really. We were given a card to enable us to have what they called 'officer status' in Cairo, or anywhere we were. It entitled us to go into all clubs, all hotels, and literally have no rank, whereas the other ranks in the other armies were not allowed access to quite a few of these clubs and restaurants.

Tell me about the clothes you were issued with.
We had a tailor-made dress uniform with leather buttons, which was quite attractive. It was a khaki wool. We also had a drill uniform which was buttoned right down the front, and a sort of cap. We were also issued with awful green lisle stockings. We called them toheroa soup stockings. There was very little coordination between Cairo and New Zealand on this subject, because we were able to take civilian clothes. We found when we got to Cairo that we were allowed to wear these things on leave but, in fact, we very rarely wore them at all. It was uniform all the way, and we were very happy to be in the uniform because it gave us all an identity and it made us feel safe when we were out. We were New Zealanders and very proud of it.

> *Pat and her 29 fellow Tuis left New Zealand on the*
> *Johann van olden Barneveldt on 15 September 1941,*
> *and duly arrived at Port Tewfik in Egypt.*

We went ashore. Lady Freyberg, who was Mrs Freyberg then, was waiting for us. We came off the ship wearing our brown felt hats and our green dress uniforms and our green toheroa stockings — hot as hell — and not knowing quite what we were going into. We were all greeted and made to feel welcome, and then we were rather concerned because we had a short distance to go to a restaurant where we were all going to have a meal and, as I remember, we were all put into an open truck like a sheep truck. We stood in it and I thought, Oh my God, is this going to be the standard? But it wasn't. It was just a short journey, and we went to this restaurant and had a nice meal. We then caught a train to Cairo and arrived in Cairo in the evening. The impact of Cairo was enormous. We tumbled out of the train feeling very, very hot in our green toheroa stockings, and Cairo station was jammed with a heaving mass of Egyptians wearing white galabiyehs and red fezzes — moving constantly, yelling, screaming, muttering. We finally were guided through this — God knows how they did this, I suppose we were shepherded like silly little lambs — to taxis, and then we were taken to the Cairo club. The drive from the station to the Cairo club itself was an adventure, because the taxis just go flat out and they honk all the time telling everyone to get out of the way. By the time we got to the Cairo club our green stockings were melting, and so were we. We were very, very tired.

The Tuis lived on the ninth floor of the building that housed the New Zealand Forces Club, and worked hard.

We were on shifts. We went downstairs to the canteen, which

was a huge room for other ranks. There were tables and chairs set all around it, and in one corner there was an ice-cream counter. The ice cream was made at Maadi by the New Zealand troops and it was fabulous. There was a tea counter where we made cups of tea and had to serve honey and toast to the troops if they felt like it. There was a cake counter, and there was an orange juice counter, where we had a great case of oranges and one orange machine, where we squeezed and squeezed and squeezed. It was quite usual to have about ten boys waiting for a glass of orange juice — just to watch us doing it, I think. And it was a very hard job. We were very tired and smothered in orange juice when we came off that machine.

Half the girls would be on duty and half the girls off duty. We worked in shifts. Half of us would be working in the kitchens preparing all the fruit salad and sending the sandwiches up in big tin cases to the little wee cake counter, keeping the canteen itself supplied with food. That was the other ranks' counter. The officers had their own dining room. New Zealand girls didn't do any cooking, so they must have had suffragis to wait on them in the dining room.

And were you doing all this work wearing your woollen uniforms?

No, no. Lady Freyberg put a stop to that straight away. In the club we wore holland uniforms. They were lovely. They buttoned down the front and we had green belts and green epaulettes with the 'New Zealand Onward' sign on them. It was a very attractive uniform. We had holland shoes with just a cross-over front, and we wore no stockings. We were very comfortable and we looked jolly good.

When we first opened it was open to all the troops in Cairo — any nationality — for a lovely fresh sandwich or ice-cream and fruit salad meal, cakes and tea. It was just a relaxing place for them to sit for hours. A lot of non-New Zealand troops found the New Zealand Forces Club and used it, and it became very popular. We became rather resentful, having to wait on them all day. Finally, when the division came down from the desert, it became so difficult for the New Zealand boys to get into the club and find seats that a decision was made to close the club to all troops except New Zealanders and Australians. It remained like that throughout the war and it became much nicer for us, too, because we were serving our own boys — and that's why we were there.

What did you see your role as in this canteen area?
Working very hard serving food, but also talking to the boys if we had time, and helping them with any ideas they had or if they wanted to know about shopping. We met lots and lots of boys and made arrangements to meet them when we were off duty. We'd come off duty at four o'clock, have a shower, and then meet them outside the club and take them shopping. The heat was tremendous, it was just like an oven outside in the streets of Cairo. But we got used to it.

Pat had warm feelings about Barbara, Lady Freyberg.

I can't stress enough how much we all loved and admired Lady Freyberg. We treated her with a great deal of respect. She was lovely, and she defended the girls and was right behind us for the whole time we were overseas. We always had her support and thoughts. When we were very busy — when the division was down — she came on [to help], particularly on the little cake counter. We were behind this rather narrow counter, and there were sandwiches in great tins behind us on a ledge and the cakes all laid out. She held these little silver tongs in her hand. The boys would be perhaps four deep, waiting to be served, and she would have her little tongs and she would say, 'Now, how can I help you?' The boys would say, 'That one', and go right down the other end and say, 'That one', and she was always so sweet. She didn't panic; her attitude never varied. But the most important thing was that she stayed there.

I remember the cake counter being very traumatic sometimes. So many boys wanted something, and some of them were not sober. I particularly remember one night I was on duty. I was serving. They were just a sea of faces, and suddenly a little Maori boy, not very old, started performing and saying, 'You never take any notice of me. You're serving everybody else. It's because I've got a brown skin.' And he berated me so much that I was crying, and I was saying, 'I'm sorry, I'll serve you now. What can I do?' He had several cousins and brothers and other Maori boys who were behind him, and they finally took him away. I was very upset and howling on the counter, but next day a group of them came in to apologise. From then on I saw them occasionally when they came down [from the desert]. They always came and spoke to me as friends, and it all turned out very well.

It is very hard to explain — it was hot, we had no cooling system. It was bedlam sometimes because there were so many faces, and it was very difficult dealing with everyone in a hurry.

The tea counter I always found awful. A whole line of boys wanting a cup of tea and two slices of toast, but we could see the point of this because General Freyberg had asked for 30 girls to go overseas to lend a touch of home and normality to the club, and he did this by staffing the big canteen with New Zealand girls in attractive uniforms. We were all young and it must have made a slight impact. I know quite a few of the boys didn't come near the club because they had other interests in Cairo, but we were always very busy and when the division came down we were inundated. We were working flat out. This was during the heat of the day, so we did work very hard. But the boys, I suppose they must have appreciated it because they always came. It was a place they knew they could come to and they would be with New Zealanders and get New Zealand food.

[In May 1943] we heard the division was coming down after the successful rout of the Germans up in the north of Africa. Three of us went out in a club jeep and stood in the sand on the edge of the desert and waited for the trucks to start arriving. And they did. Truck after truck after truck of tired, dirty, grim-looking men came, and we waved and waved and waved. It was a very moving moment for me, [seeing] the division coming down straight out of battle.

Later that year the *Tuis* moved to Italy.

There were lots of reinforcements on the ship from New Zealand going to join the division in Italy. At night we had blackout. It was quite eerie in the very stillness of the night — brilliant stars and the swishing of the water against the sides of the ship.

On deck a group of girls and New Zealand troops all gathered, and they were teaching us songs that we hadn't heard of. One of them took my fancy; it went, 'Don't sit under the apple tree with anybody else but me, anybody else but me, anybody else but me. Oh no, no, don't sit under the apple tree with anybody else but me, till I come marching home.' That's a moment that I have never forgotten.

We arrived at Taranto and then we were driven by truck to Bari, which was very bleak; a cold, poor town. It was on the coast of the Adriatic, and it was poverty-stricken and very bleak. The club was all right, but it was cold and we didn't like it very much. We were all in one big dormitory instead of three rooms, so every time anyone came in off duty at twelve o'clock, they woke everyone up. It was not very satisfactory.

However, we were happy there, and we did establish a club and went back to the same routine of making sandwiches and food for the boys. [It was] a New Zealand base not too far away from Cassino, where the most awful fight was raging. The troops would come down for a week's leave, a few trucks at a time. We would be waiting outside the doors for them to arrive, waving them in, and then the male members of staff would issue them with clean clothing and hot baths and show them their rooms, and then they would come in and eat sandwiches or whatever we had to offer them. It was very moving, because we were so close to the war and we could see the impact it had made on the boys. It was cold, and it was a different sort of war — mud and snow and slush.

They stayed a week, and in that time we'd take them on picnics to lovely little bays south of Bari. We would take trestle tables and lots of food and cut sandwiches. We'd go in the trucks and the boys, when we reached the spot, would go haring all over the countryside looking for what they called 'rooster's blood' or 'plonk'. It was a red wine, but very newly brewed and not very nice. They would sit in big groups drinking this plonk, and we would be making sandwiches. We all swam, and then we wandered around among the boys and sat and talked to them and drank wine. I particularly loved watching Lady Freyberg going from group to group. She was so immaculate and dainty, and she would go up to a group of half-tiddly Kiwis who were all in a good, jovial mood and they would say, 'Have a drink, Mrs Freyberg,' and she would say, 'Thank you.' She would drink this dreadful stuff and say, 'That was delicious!' and move on to the next group. How many wines she hid behind her back and spilled into the sand or how many wines she drank, I don't know, but I think that was the most obvious way of seeing how hard she worked.

The night before they left, we had a dance in the building and invited the nurses and VADs and sisters who were there. It was really very nice. The next morning, early, we would all be up in the kitchen making cups of tea and sandwiches to start them on their way, and wave them off as they went off in their trucks back to Cassino, to the battle.

It was a very poverty-stricken town — little kids barefooted — and it had felt the impact of the war. My memories of Bari should stay with me because that's where I met Peter Hamilton, who married me. I was on duty in the Bari club one night — it was a cold, bleak night — and this slightly wobbly young officer came in with a rather shy grin and came up to the counter. I had met him casually in Cairo once or twice; it hadn't meant a thing to me. He said, 'It's my birthday.' He had just come down from Cassino and he had a week's leave. He obviously came in to see if he could find someone in the club who would go out with him.

I got off duty and I went with him to the [Hotel] Imperiali, where he sat in a sort of bewildered muse and I danced most of the evening with a young Maori officer, who was a most wonderful dancer. Peter was quite happy, he was just sitting there half asleep. He finally went back to the division, and very shortly after that he arrived back in Bari. He was being sent to the senior officers' course in Haifa for six months. He stayed for a little time in Bari and in that time we fell in love and became engaged. He set off for Cairo and bought me a beautiful diamond solitaire ring, and Dick Pemberton, one of the engineer officers, brought it back and gave it to me with great aplomb in the club sitting room in Bari. We were engaged.

Although they were not near the front line, the dangers of war still came close for the Tuis in Bari.

We were upstairs in our big dormitory one night when we heard this enormous explosion down near the harbour. We went to the window, sat on the floor and watched this horrific scene of American ships in the Bari harbour being bombed by the German air force. There were Very lights and flashlights, it was like an enormous fireworks display, but it was terrible because the ships there had mustard gas on board. A lot of the boys jumped into the water and they were all badly burned. They were taken to our hospital, just out of Bari, and there the New Zealand nursing sisters and VADs took them in and cared for them.

We were upstairs watching, quite unaware of the danger. Bill Smith, our RSM at the club, a very nice guy, came up to the dormitory and said, 'Get downstairs, you girls. Into the cellar,' which we did, rapidly. Apart from the fact that it was a horrific evening, it was quite comical because one of the girls had forgotten her false teeth, another one had her hair in curlers, and we were all in various stages of undress. The next morning we really came down to earth with a great thud, because the aftermath of it all was pretty terrible and there were lots of very sick boys in the hospital.

After Rome fell to the Allies, a New Zealand Forces Club was established in the city.

General Freyberg rushed into Rome and took possession of the Hotel Quirinale, which was one of the big hotels in Rome. Six of us from Bari went up to the Rome club. I shared a room with Christine Farrer; it was a beautiful room with a telephone beside the bed. It backed onto a courtyard. The building on the opposite side was the Rome opera house, and we could lie in our bed in our room and listen to opera all evening if we wished to. It was an amazing change. Rome was so very beautiful.

We staffed the information desk. In the club at the time we had two young Roman Catholic priests who were New Zealanders who happened to be in the Vatican, training, when war broke out with Italy. They were Father Sneddon and Father Flanagan. They knew Rome very well, so they organised trips and sightseeing for the boys who came down on leave. These same boys who had rioted around Cairo, all turned up in Rome to go to the opera and sightseeing. It was quite a revelation to me that so many of them did this and did enjoy the opera.

We didn't have any mundane duties, because this was a luxury hotel and the [Italian] staff was kept on. They did all the cooking and making beds. I didn't meet any of them except a Swiss man who had been with the hotel for some time. I grew to love him, and it was he who arranged for us to go to a pensione in Rome [on] the night of our wedding. He gave us the most beautiful little silver cake spatula. It was delicately wrought and very beautiful, and I treasure it still.

In late October 1944, Peter Hamilton returned from Haifa for their wedding on 30 October.

I found an Italian dressmaker and she made me some exquisite little undies. I paid her with bully beef and spam and fruitcake — food, rather than money, because they didn't need money but they were desperately short of food. She was very kind to me. She let me use her wedding gown. It was a beautiful gown, white, and it had layer upon layer of tulle to the ground. She also gave me her veil to wear. I was very lucky, and I loved her for doing this.

Two of Pat's fellow Tuis were her bridesmaids.

So the wedding day arrived. The club cook had made a huge wedding cake from cakes we supplied from New Zealand. We got them from other girls who had them, and maybe we got some from the New Zealand base. The cook made a tiered cake and he was very proud of it. We were married in the Anglican church, All Saints, in Rome. Father Sneddon became very enthusiastic about our wedding and organised an ex-Sistine Choir singer to sing at the wedding. [He also] organised the Irish Free State limousine. It was a huge black car, very lavish, and it had the green flag flying on the front. We really would have preferred to go to the wedding in a battered old divisional truck, but we didn't want to hurt his feelings, so we set out from the club in this Irish Free State car with the green flag flying. It caused a few raised eyebrows from the boys standing round outside the club, I think.

The reason for this, Pat remarked, was that the Irish Free State was neutral, but 'not very friendly'.

The day before the wedding Colonel Anderson, who was the CO of the Divisional Engineers at the time, came down with all Peter's friends. On the way they called in at a farm and got some geese. They chased these geese round and round a haystack, but they finally caught two and paid the Italians for them, and then they continued on their trip down to Rome.

The wedding reception was held in the Forces Club at the Hotel Quirinale. I don't recall much about it. We had cold goose as part of the celebrations, and when Peter and I left to go to the pensione for the night we took a large lump of cold goose with us. I remember this dim little pensione with candlelight. We sat on the bed and ate cold goose and drank wine. The next day we set off for Positano, which is south of Naples.

After their marriage, Pat and Peter returned to their respective units. In early May 1945, the Germans surrendered in Italy.

We were down at a lovely picnic spot which was utterly deserted. We were sitting quietly munching a sandwich when we heard church bells ringing in the distance, and over the hill came a sole English soldier absolutely running his heart out, his arms wide-stretched, shouting, 'It's peace, it's peace!' We both sat there absolutely dumbfounded; Peter had tears in his eyes. The next morning we went back to the club. Once we were inside the building we were not allowed out again. Everyone was confined to quarters because there might be repercussions round the village. That night we had a big dinner and a dance on the roof of the club. Everyone tried to be bright and gay, but it was a very sad occasion. I can remember sitting in a chair and Peter sitting on the ground with his head in my lap, crying. It was an enormous reaction. He just felt and remembered all the boys that he had known and liked so much who were not celebrating it with him.

Pat was soon pregnant with their first child, Elizabeth, and went to Cairo, where Peter joined her to wait for a ship back to New Zealand.

The moment I stepped on board the ship, the *Strathaird*, I put the East behind me and we returned back to our beloved country, New Zealand, and our family.

Pat's return to New Zealand in 1945 was a short one. After the birth of her daughter in March 1946 she joined Peter in Batu Gajah, Malaya, where he had found a job as a mining inspector for the Colonial Service. Her life with Peter was one of creating homes in new places as his work in Malaya, and then with the regular New Zealand Army, required them to make frequent moves. Their marriage, begun in wartime Italy, was a happy one.

Of the three clubs you were involved in, Bari, Rome and Cairo, which one do you remember the most?

I have the greatest affection for Cairo. I can never forget the impact of Cairo. We were filled with, naive, I suppose, hopes to do good. We were very, very proud of what we had been chosen for, and we hoped that we would make a good job of it. I truly think we did, although we had a lot of criticism. It was mooted abroad that we were 'officer-conscious' and that we would never go out with the boys. Well, it may have happened with some of the girls, but I didn't come in contact with many officers. Most of the boys from my home town were other ranks. When I was off duty I went out with who I liked and did things I wanted.

I think in Cairo we certainly made a difference to the canteen where they came and had their food, but I wouldn't go any further than that. Maybe we contributed a little bit of home to the atmosphere, but I could never be confident in saying that we made all that amount of difference to them. We just liked to feel we did.

'I MET AN ITALIAN GIRL'

GORDON JOHNSTON, 63740, PRIVATE, 5 FIELD REGIMENT

Gordon Johnston was born in Port Chalmers in February 1919. He grew up in Port Chalmers, attending school there and at Otago Boys' High School. After leaving school he trained as a teacher and spent a year in Auckland doing a special study on physical education. It was as he was travelling back to Dunedin that he and his friends heard that war had been declared.

I THINK WE WERE AT Taumarunui when war was declared. It didn't mean anything much to me, it didn't really sink in. I had decided that I'd like to be a doctor, so I went to varsity and did medical intermediate. That was in 1940.

He had tried to join up in 1939.

I told them my age, and I don't know why they told me I was too young, because lots of people were younger than me, but they maybe didn't say so. But anyhow, that sealed my fate. I completed the medical intermediate course and would normally have gone into medical school the following year, but I was called up. The question then was which field I'd go into. My brother was at this stage training to be an air force pilot and, I don't know why, but I said I'd go in the army.

As a medical student, Gordon would not have had to join the armed forces.

If you were a medical student you were automatically exempt. I've never regretted that, actually. The family had all lined me up for being a doctor, and I was quite keen, but I have never regretted it.

Gordon was sent to Papakura Camp near Auckland to train in the artillery. He did not enjoy his training much.

We did three months of marching up and down, using rifles. I had a lot of fun, but it didn't grab me as a thing to be doing. We didn't have any guns. I think there might have been an 18-pounder, but basically the training was either paper training or marching.

Gordon's troop of artillery was kept behind to keep the camp going for the new intake.

I was saved from that three months of doing nothing, more or less, [because] they wanted to set up a survey group. They called for people who had studied mathematics to a higher level, so I thought, Well, I'll get out of this. So I volunteered for the survey group and I spent the next three months training in survey. We had to work out our positions from the stars and we did some really interesting, useful work. I left [New Zealand] with the next lot as a potential army surveyor, still attached to the artillery.

Gordon returned to Port Chalmers for his final leave. His parents did not tell him their feelings about having another son go overseas to the war.

My brother was training in Canada, and Mum was sorry to lose another one of her boys, and she had lost her brother in the other war, so no doubt she was pretty worried. But they were great. We didn't have a send-off party in Port Chalmers, we had a private one at home. We had a pool table, and the family and one or two friends played pool and we had a private family farewell. I was quite excited about the whole prospect, because although casualty lists were coming and we'd lost Crete, until a thing's actually in your experience you don't know, so I was glad to be away. That first three months made me want to get somewhere.

Gordon left New Zealand in the Seventh Reinforcements on the Aquitania *at the end of 1941 as one of a group of around 30 surveyors.*

I was on Deck H. It was so hot down below we were allowed to hang the [hammocks] up on the deck. It was nice sleeping there. [Indian deckhands] would come along at about five o'clock: 'Wakey, wakey. Washy decky! Wakey wakey, washy decky!' If you didn't get out, you got wet. So that was a good wake-up.

The ship's destination in Egypt was Port Said. Before we arrived, on board ship, we had talks by three or four different people. One was the padre, and he told us that we'd be faced with a lot of temptations and [we should] remember our principles and all this sort of thing. Then there was a doctor and he said, 'When you get to Cairo, make your first trip to the Museum of Hygiene, because there you will see what will happen to you if you get venereal disease.' And everybody, every New Zealander, went to the Museum of Hygiene. It had all sorts of things in bottles. Shocking things. It was a bit scary, I suppose.

And then the sergeant — he was a guy who'd been in the first war, I think; he was an older fellow — he said, 'Whatever these other guys say, don't you take any notice of them. You're going to do it.' And he gave us instructions of how to avoid getting venereal disease. So that was our introduction to Cairo.

Gordon joined Don Troop of 28 Battery of 5 Field Regiment as an observation post truck driver. At the time, the Alamein Line was being set up. As he was in Don (or D) Troop, the truck was called the R Don truck — 'R' stood for Reconnaissance.

The captain's job, especially when we were static, was to go up in a wee truck. There were four of us altogether and our job was to go as close to the enemy as we could, or where we could see something to shoot at. The driver of R Don, which was this O Pip truck, he'd had enough. He'd been in since the

Second Ech and he wasn't going back any more, so I landed his job. I became the O Pip, observation post, driver till we got to Tripoli. And I was very happy to do that. I had a nice feeling of being master of my own destiny — nobody really was in the army but, up to a certain point, I felt I was.

When the regiment reached Tripoli, Gordon's commanding officer was given an armoured car.

The colonel, Gussie Glasgow, whom I knew — he had taught me at high school (he was the chemistry master) and at university — asked me if I would come and drive his armoured car. I said, 'Gussie, I belong to Don Troop.' He said, 'I would like you to because we can talk about old times in Dunedin.' He was probably lonely. He said, 'Any time you want to go back to your troop, I'll fix it.' So I did that. I got this armoured car. It was a big brute of a thing. He had a jeep, which he travelled in, and if things got a bit sticky, he would get in the armoured car and go forward to see what decisions he had to make.

After the desert campaign finished and the division returned to Maadi Camp, Colonel Glasgow was promoted and Gordon drove the armoured car for his successor as regimental commander, Colonel Leonard Thornton. Gordon's ambition had always been to drive an artillery quad, and so he asked to be transferred back to Don Troop. It was only when Colonel Glasgow visited the regiment in Italy that Gordon was able to achieve this ambition.

He strode up the hill, took his red hat off and threw it on the ground and sat down, and we had a good old yarn about how he was doing and so on. We yarned away, and that's when I told him that Colonel Thornton wouldn't let me go back to the troop. He said, 'You're back to the troop tomorrow.' So that's how I got back to Don Troop, 28 Battery. When I went back again, there were only four quad drivers and nobody was going to move over for me, so I was given a jeep and was what they call a DR, a despatch rider. In the first war they used to use motorbikes and we used them a bit, but basically jeeps took that over. So I did that for some time until the Fifth Reinforcements went home. And then I got my quad. That was halfway up Italy somewhere.

Tell me what a quad is.

The quad itself was very high and stumpy. They were sometimes called beetles because they were quite high off the ground and had a very short chassis. It had to carry six gunners and the driver inside, so it had a lot of storage space. Behind it there was a thing called a limber, which carried all the ammunition. It was a little trailer. And behind that was the gun itself. So when you were on the move you had all the gun crew in the quad, and the limber and the gun behind. The quad was a very powerful thing. It was a four-wheel drive, and it had a winch so that if you got stuck — which we did in Italy quite a lot — you winched the gun or whatever. It was one of the great vehicles of the war, and we had those right from the start of the war. They had very powerful engines, mostly Chevs.

We fired a lot of stuff [at the Senio River] but we got caught shortly afterwards by the snow. We got snowbound. The

Germans couldn't move; we couldn't move. Most of the guys got either into bivvies or into casas, but I had this armoured car. How did we keep warm? We had a tin with charcoal in and a couple of bits of wire on it, and you poured a bit of petrol on and lit it. It would keep going, but the charcoal would die down, so every now and then you had to get out and give it a swing round to get a bit of air in it. At night time you'd look out over where the Div was, and you'd see these things swinging round. This particular armoured car had a hole in the floor. It was a steel floor and I've never ever worked out what that hole was for, but I found out that if you put your charcoal burner on top of that, the air coming through kept it going. [Jack Blyth] was a signaller and was with me. At the worst of the snow we would sit in there with this burner. Then one night he just keeled over. I guessed what had happened right away. It was darn carbon monoxide. So I opened the door — it was snowed up, of course — and I pushed him out in the snow, and eventually he recovered.

Gordon remembers the battle at Cassino.

We had a grandstand view. We were right beside it and saw the Americans smash the place to smithereens. Bomb after bomb. They were terrible for bombing, the Americans. They'd bomb anywhere. We saw that and it was dramatic, but what we didn't take part in, of course, was the infantry crossing of the Rapido [River]. That was a pretty dramatic thing for the infantry involved, but not for me.

A mate of mine was killed there. We were going through a place and there were some cabbages in a paddock, so he hopped out and went over and picked a cabbage up, and it was booby-trapped and he was killed. He was one of a family of seven boys, and they were all killed.

It was such a different war from Africa because there were houses, there were people, there were animals, and all that sort of thing. We were holed up at one spot and just behind us there was an underground dugout that had been built for some while, and I heard that there was a French family there. So I went to see them and there was a couple with their two children, two girls, and they had been there right through the German [occupation], and they were living underground. We got on because I could speak French. [The husband] had to go somewhere and he was scared to leave his wife. He thought she might be interfered with some way or other. We were in a static line at the time so whenever I could, I went back — it was only about a hundred yards, I suppose — and stayed with them while he went away. Goodness knows what he was doing. That family eventually survived. They went to America and wrote to me, sent me a photo of their family. So that was a nice thing.

We were at Florence, above the River Arno, and we saw the Germans smash all the bridges, six of them. They didn't smash the [Ponte Vecchio], they broke the buildings down near the end of it.

Gordon did not get into Florence at this time, but visited later on leave.

There were a few factories open by this time. I went to a place where they had porcelain or glass and wee boys, just kids, twelve years old, sitting in a row, would paint the most beautiful things on it. Flowers. They would paint it with a grey paint which I eventually worked out was zinc, and then they would put it in a furnace and bake it on, then they would put it in a silver bath and the silver would replace the zinc. I brought a glass thing home for my mum done in that style.

When we got to the River Po the Germans had blown up all the bridges and to get across, the Engineers had built a temporary bridge, a pontoon. But to get onto it, you came down and you had to turn at right angles. I was Don 3, number 3, so there were two in front of me and when they went onto the bridge, they backed and round, and backed and round, and eventually got on. I said to the guys, 'I'm going straight over. Are you OK?' Because if I missed, they wouldn't be OK. I went down and I drove on and the sergeant got out and watched. I drove on and we went across. He told me I had half the front tyre just over the edge of the wood. But I got over in one swoop. I guess I wanted to do this as I was the oldest driver — show-off me!

Old Freyberg grabbed the most important hotels all through Italy. He did this in Rome, he did it everywhere. He grabbed the Badiglione Hotel in Florence, and one night they put a concert on for the people that were there on leave from the army. They invited local people. One girl came on one night. She wasn't very pretty, she was nicely built but she wasn't attractive in that sense, but she sang 'Ave Maria', and I tell you the guys there, they were all in tears. They wouldn't let her go. What a gorgeous voice. All the Kiwis were very homesick at that stage.

In Italy we were going through their country and it was

tragic half the time. It was terrible. At mess time we'd have a tin and we'd be eating and here's not only kids but young people, standing there with their tins. And the jokers would eat some of their meal and then they'd give the rest to them. Italy wasn't a good place to have a war. The animals, you'd see them lying dead. All the houses around were bombed. We had to knock them down because the enemy could hide behind them or in them or under them. This happened all through our advance in Italy.

On another occasion we were in a wee village and the Italians — they know all their operas — and they put one on for the New Zealand Div as we went through. Right up in the gods, the Italians were allowed in. When it was over, they kept yelling out 'Più! Più! Più!', which means 'More! More! More!' We thought they were booing. We were prepared to throw them out till someone realised that what they were saying was 'More!'

Did much looting go on?

Not really, not really, because mostly we didn't go through big cities and we were on the move most of the time. We sidetracked Rome, we sidetracked Florence — well, we didn't pause in Florence — so for three quarters of the way up Italy, they were just villages and smallish places. There may have been some looting. When we were in Florence we were on the hills over the Arno, and we must have been there for about a week, I think. The houses were big beautiful homes and, of course, they were mostly pro-German. They were Italians, but they had been supporters of the Fascists, so they were empty. They had either taken what they had or they hid what they couldn't take, and I know some people — one of our troop, actually, he broke in and took a whole lot of stuff. I would say that, by and large, bad looting was rare. I don't know that we were especially angelic or anything, but we didn't have the opportunity. You always get people — they might be good people but everybody's got somewhere or other, a kernel of naughtiness — but basically the New Zealanders were a pretty good lot, apart from some people. So any looting would be done by people when we were in static conditions, more than anything else.

What about trading then?
We didn't have anything to trade. All we had to trade was food or cigarettes. I traded all my cigarettes because I didn't smoke.

I didn't ever go into a person's house and stay, even in the snow, but quite a lot of guys would go in. It was always very amicable. They were always very pleased even though most of their animals were killed. They'd have all their things hanging from the ceiling, all their vegetables. Some of the guys learned to speak Italian, especially the Maoris. They were pretty good at it. But usually we weren't in any place for any length of time. A couple of nights. If some people saw a chook, they would take their chooks and at Christmas, perhaps a pig. There was a bit of that sort of stuff, but it wasn't widespread. They had very little.

Tell me about coming into Trieste.
I was still driving my quad. We'd crossed the River Po. We knew that there was a big race on, that the Yugoslavs were trying

to get into Trieste before us, so once we'd crossed the Po we went like mad. When our regiment got to Trieste, there were Yugoslavs there. They had come in just about the same time. Our troop were sent up to a little village on the top of the hills, Aurisina, and our job was to stop any more Yugoslavs coming down into Trieste. What was happening down in Trieste was that the Yugoslavs didn't want to move out. After a few days I got into Trieste and I saw our tanks lined up in the square, all facing where the Yugoslavs were. They moved out. I don't care what the experts say, the fact that Trieste remained in Italy was due to the New Zealanders. Guarantee it.

We were up there in the hills and the Yugoslavs were across the street from us. They were laden with grenades, women and all. They were very, very scruffy — poor people. We controlled the main road. They didn't seem to be interested. We talked to them. One of our fellas had a violin and it had been damaged. One of these Yugoslavs knew what to do, and he tied it up with a whole lot of stuff and glued it up. He had his violin back again. It was amicable. We couldn't speak their language and they couldn't speak our language. After about three or four days we could see that they weren't interested in coming down, so I thought I'd better go down and see what the city was like, which I did.

After the New Zealanders arrived in Trieste and the war was over, many activities were organised to keep the troops occupied. One of these was a rowing regatta for which Gordon volunteered. The 5 Field Regiment took over a cantoniera or rowing club built out over the Adriatic so that the men could train, which they did in the morning and late afternoon when it was not too hot.

I thought I'd go on an exploration, and I went all the way around to a private bathing establishment, called a savoia. It was out of bounds to troops, they had sentries on, and inside they had cabins and structures built out over the Adriatic. You could sunbathe on these wharf-like things and swim. I thought, Gee, I want to get in there. There were some New Zealand sentries, but they weren't on duty there. I went over to them and I said to these guys — because I had my identity discs on — I said, 'Could I strip off here?' 'Yes, OK,' they replied. So I stripped off. I had a bathing suit and I was as brown as a berry, I got my towel, left my gear there and I walked up to these Tommy sentries and straight through them, didn't take any notice of them. I looked like an Italian.

There were people everywhere. There were three girls sitting near one place, and one of them asked me for a match. These were three nurses from the hospital. I liked the look of one of them especially. I couldn't speak Italian — I'd picked up the odd words — but the three of them could speak French, so we yarned away in French. I wanted to know one of them a bit more.

I went there every day for a while and Luciana and I got very cobbery. I had to take the three of them everywhere. I wanted one of them to be by herself, but these two others came. Eventually I wrote home and told my parents that I had met an Italian girl who I liked very much. My mum wrote back and pointed out all the problems with marrying. You see, they were old-fashioned and my mother's brother had married a

Catholic person and had had a terrible life. It used to happen, and they were worried about that. But by the time her reply came, we had already become engaged.

I went to ask her mother if I could marry her — her father was wounded in the first war and he died afterwards, in about 1923, I think. I had to ask the mother, and of course the mother couldn't speak English. I couldn't speak Italian and she couldn't speak French. So here's Luciana and her mother and me and I asked her if I could marry Luciana. Luciana asked the mother, and I always maintain that the mother said no and Luciana said yes.

The war was over, and lots of New Zealanders had met Italian girls and the New Zealand Army thought that it wasn't a very good idea. Guys had been away from female company for a long time and it'd be much better if they didn't get married. So they laid a law down that if any New Zealand soldier wanted to pair up with an Italian lady, they would give priority to go to New Zealand to engaged couples.

So Luciana and I went to the major. He was an Englishman, head of AMGOT, who'd been appointed major of Trieste. He produced a document signifying that he engaged us, and he signed it and put his stamp on it and all that. I took it back and they then said, 'You've got to send that to New Zealand.' I happened to know the Minister of Defence, who was Fred Jones. He was from St Kilda and I sent it to him. He said, 'I'll fix it for you.' He did that, so when there were ten [prospective] brides who were on the first ship, Luciana was one of those. That's how it all happened.

The other thing was that you had to get to New Zealand yourself first and then claim. I was due to go home months prior to this. I went down to Bari, ready to go home, and had a long stay there, an unpleasant stay, actually, because we were out in tents in sand and it was a very unpleasant place. I was thinking of Luciana up in Trieste, so I went to the CO. I said, 'Look, I want to go back to Trieste.' He said, 'You're on home leave. You can't go.' I said, 'I'm going. If you like to give me a ticket of some sort that might be useful, you can, but I'm going anyway.' So he gave me one.

I went out to the airport, slept in a ditch that night, [and the next morning found a] South African plane called a Matador that had come down from somewhere to pick up wine. There were two pilots and me, and a whole lot of wine. I hitch-hiked back to Trieste.

Gordon got back to New Zealand in September 1945.

I bought a translation set, *How to Speak Italian,* and I studied that so by the time Luciana came we could forget our French and speak Italian. Luciana arrived in February 1946. They left Trieste and they zigzagged down Italy, picking up different war brides till they got to the ship. She had to wait in Bari for a long time. They had a married lady, Mrs Tanner, in charge of them, and she was very good to them. The people on the ship were also very good to them.

My sister came with me to bring Luciana down from Lyttelton. We were waiting on the wharf when the ship came in, and it was having trouble berthing because the waves were quite big. My sister and I were standing there, and there were these girls, waving. My sister said, 'There's one there. She's waving. That must be her.' I said, 'That's not her. She's not there!' Luciana had got cold feet and she was down in the cabin.

She didn't get homesick until they called in at Fremantle, and it was at Fremantle that she felt she wanted to go home. My parents were wonderful, and the rest of the family. Luciana arrived and caused a great deal of interest in Port Chalmers and what was fascinating, lovely for Luciana, was that they all took her to heart. Although we had been fighting the Italians, there was no anti [feeling]. I sometimes say to her, 'It was a great thing to leave all your family and come here to a country where you couldn't even speak the language.' And customs and that. She cooked different food — not nowadays, because everyone eats Italian nowadays. So it was a wonderful thing, and I often think of that.

Gordon and Luciana married in 1946. He returned to teaching after getting an MSc from Otago University, and ended up lecturing at Dunedin Teachers' College. Luciana tutored in Italian at Otago Polytechnic.

'I HAD A PRETTY CHARMED LIFE'

Reginald MINTER, 620068, Private, 24 Battalion

Reg Minter was born in Auckland in 1923. After he left Northcote High School he became an apprentice electroplater. He joined a sapper unit of the Territorials in June 1940, was called up after the Japanese attack on the Pearl Harbor naval base in December 1941, and went overseas with the Tenth Reinforcements in July 1943. He was not needed by the Divisional Engineers, so he and a friend tossed a coin to see if they would join the artillery (Reg's preference) or the infantry. Reg's friend won, and together they joined 24 Battalion at Maadi Camp.

THEY WANTED REGIMENTAL SIGNALLERS FOR the battalion. We both agreed on this. We volunteered for Regimental Signals and did a two-month course in Maadi under our New Zealand Divisional Signals School. They had quite a big school there. They had rooms with Morse code and radios to practise on — things like procedure in radio, netting in your radio.

Being a regimental sig, you had your own sig platoon and battalion, and three signalmen were seconded to each rifle company, to Company Headquarters. I was seconded to B Company, then later on I spent about eleven months with A Company. Eventually I was the chief signaller there. You had a chief sig, then you had two others. You were all the same rank, but you were classed a Leading Signalman in that little group of signallers.

The New Zealand Division went to Italy in October 1943.

We didn't finish our course till November. We had Christmas Day in Maadi, then the next day we were on the train to Alexandria, where we caught a ship to go over to Italy.

It only took us three or four days. We landed at Taranto and went to Advanced Base, which was just south of Bari. A very old, ancient medieval town, that was. We stayed there about two or three weeks, then we shot up and joined our battalion. The Sangro River had been crossed and they were pulling out of Orsogna when I joined the battalion. I was with Battalion Headquarters. Then the whole Div moved over to the other side of Italy to prepare us for Cassino. We didn't know that at the time.

We went to a little place called Alife, and that's when we first met the Yanks. They brought their big mobile shower along. It must have taken about four huge trucks, and there was a series of tents. They were well-organised. You went to your shower, and at the other end you had all-new underclothing. That was the only hot shower I had in three years, during the whole time I was in Italy. We had Benghazi burners. They were made of a round cylinder like a long can, and in it, it had a funnel.

It went up like a little chimney. You filled the outer part with water; it had a spout on it. It used to sit over a little tin. You put petrol in the tin, lit it, and put the can over the top, and that's how we boiled water. It was quite quick. That's what we used to shave and wash with. In the summer time, of course, we washed in cold water. You had no opportunities [to wash properly] while you were in the line, apart from washing your face and feet. I always used to like washing my feet. They used to laugh at me.

How did you find Italy after Egypt?
Well, the climate was a lot nicer, although the first time I ever saw snow was in Italy. The first lot of snow was before they pulled out of Orsogna. There was quite a lot of snow there.

We were in pretty poor areas. Real peasant country. Italy's an old country, and the villages appeared very old to us. It was quite educating for us young guys, seeing these old places. Actually, we didn't realise at the time just how significant it was, all the historical things we were looking at. We didn't really grasp what they really were.

Tell me about going into battle for the first time. Where was that?
The real first one for me was Cassino. We shifted over to Cassino. Before we went into the actual area, for about a week we were just a few miles behind Cassino near what used to be a railway line, but they'd pulled the railway lines up and made it like a road. We took over from the Yanks — I think it was their 34 Division. By this time, I'd been seconded to B Company from Battalion Headquarters. Major Turnbull was

the company commander — he was a good officer, too.

24 was reserve battalion, but B Company was seconded to 25 Battalion to make an extra-strong battalion. They had an extra rifle company, which was us. After the big barrage, everybody moved back a couple of miles. The poor old Americans, they bombed everywhere. It was mooted that some of the bombers were staunch Catholics and didn't want to bomb the place because of the monastery, but I don't know, I think that was just gossip.

However, at five o'clock our company went in. We went along the Rapido River. The bombing had diverted the river and it flooded the botanical gardens in Cassino. Unfortunately, they had [put down] S-mines, and you couldn't see them, because it was covered in water. We weren't in that particular strip but 26 Battalion were, and they had a lot of casualties. However, we went in — at five o'clock at night. I've always wondered whether I was on Gaumont British News, because Gaumont British News was there photographing us as we were going along the edge of the river.

Just as we got in there it started to rain. One of our platoons got lost — it was black as anything. There were plenty of flares and that going up, but it was complete confusion because there was so much devastation in the town that there were no roads or anything. Everybody was just groping for what location we were in. We went into a big broken building, and it wasn't very nice there because some Germans had been caught with the bombs and [there was] quite a lot of mess, so we moved out of that building until we got to the post office.

We stayed there that night. One of our platoons went up to the right of us and had a bit of a battle there. They lost two or three guys. A couple of guys got decorated there, for wiping out quite a few of the enemy.

From there, we stayed put. We couldn't get any radio contact at all. Our radios looked very flashy and modern, but they didn't have very much power, really. Their range was fairly limited, especially if you had big broken buildings that screened [the signal], so we were at a loss for a while.

That was the night of 15 March 1944. On the sixteenth, we were there all day in that rubble.

Was there fighting going on outside in the town?
Yes, but during the day there wasn't much because we were sending a lot of smoke shells to try and hide us, because you could see the Germans walking around the perimeter of the monastery. You couldn't move during the day. He had snipers all over the place.

'He' was the Germans, or 'Ted'. Tedeschi, that was the Italian name. Very rarely did we call them Germans. It was always Ted, always the Teds.

There was a bit of broken rubble, so Aussie [the chief signaller] said, 'We'll carry the set up there.' There was a big wall beside it, just on its own. We couldn't get any reception there so we brought [the radio] over, and as soon as we left the whole wall collapsed, so good job we did. It just collapsed, and that noise brought a bit of shelling onto us. Still, we were quite safe in the post office.

That was on the sixteenth. On the seventeenth, we moved up towards the crypt. We advanced a bit more. On the eighteenth, in the morning, we went about 30 or 50 yards. By this time they'd got the tanks across into the town. We had two tanks coming up to join us. The sergeant major said, 'We'd better dig in or get into these holes.' He'd no sooner said that when a machine gun opened up on us. One of my sigs got a nasty burst right down the side of his leg. Poor bugger, he did scream, too. I had the telephone and that received about three bullets instead of me, so that was all right. I had a pretty charmed life.

We went further on, then we met the tanks. What happened then? Oh yes, in the back of the tank there's a socket and a little phone you can pick up. The company commander picked up the phone and spoke to the commander of the tank inside. We were going to try and advance and see if we could take the Continental Hotel. I suppose we went about 40 yards and all hell broke loose. That's when me and several others got hit.

By shrapnel?

Mmm. I ended up on my face. Something just picked me up and threw me down. I didn't know I'd been hit. Never felt a thing. I had my boss's Italian sub-machine gun. They were quite nice. Instead of metal, it had a wooden butt, and I looked down and that butt had been smashed. Merv, the Company Sergeant Major said, 'Are you all right?' I said, 'Yeah. I think so.'

I went to stand up and I fell down again, my leg wouldn't work. I got a hell of a shock. I looked at it to see if I still had it. My right leg. The shrapnel had gone into it and put my leg into shock. It just wasn't working. I saw a tear and I put my hand down inside my thigh and felt blood. I thought, Oh, hell. Shorty Walker, our medic, said, 'You'd better get back to the crypt.' Just opposite the post office was a sort of a church, and it had a big crypt underneath. Our own battalion doctor had come up, probably to help the 25 Battalion doctor, and they'd created a little first-aid post down in the crypt. Shorty said to me, 'Can you get back there?' I said, 'Yeah, I think so.' The reason he asked me if I could get back there on my own was because we had several more seriously wounded than myself who needed attention. I had to walk about 150 yards. But I couldn't walk, so I dragged myself. Shorty said, 'I'll come back. Try and make your way there and I'll come back and get you.' I said, 'OK.' I got about halfway and there was a huge bomb hole there, and I don't know why but something made me listen. I could hear this scream come over, so I crawled down in the side of the bomb hole. And all hell broke loose. The shells must have been pretty close.

About four shells landed and then it stopped. I crawled up. [Shorty] got hold of me, helped me up and I hopped along with one leg and we got into the crypt.

I didn't feel a thing at that particular stage, it was still numb. It was just as if someone had given me an inoculation to deaden the whole leg. Doc Borrie had a look at it and he said, 'That's gone right in, but it's made a nice little neat hole.' Some of 26 Battalion were there too. God, some of them, poor boys, they were hit bad with these mines. About an hour later, it did start to ache. One of the medical sergeants said, 'How's your leg?' I said, 'It's starting to ache now.' He said, 'I'm going to give you a shot of morphine in the leg.' Which he did.

The trouble was, we couldn't get out during the daytime. It was impossible. There were too many snipers, and they'd mortar you or machine-gun you, so everything had to happen at night. I was there the whole day and all the next day, and I got out the following night.

How did you get out?

Good question! I couldn't have walked a mile through all that rubble, but I cannot remember being carried out in a stretcher. And yet I must have [been].

When I was in the crypt there was another battalion guy, a corporal. He said, 'Reg, put this on.' It was a German overcoat, fur-lined. Beautiful and warm — because I was getting shivers now and then. Shock, I suppose.

When I got to the other end, into a proper RAP, I looked a mess. All this masonry and bombing, rain. It was like chalk, and I was covered as if somebody had put chalk all over me. I could have been anybody. I was sitting there on a stool, waiting.

It was a long time before Reg was seen to because the men at the Regimental Aid Post thought he was German.

Because of the coat. I had no other signature at all, just a big long coat and boots. Then I was taken to the Casualty Clearing Station. The battalion had a jeep with stretchers on each side — they'd just slide you on your stretcher on to the jeep. From there, I went right to Caserta, which is just north of Naples, to our 2 General Hospital. They were very busy, naturally, because all our casualties went into 2GH because our other hospital was way down the bottom of Italy. They had a look at me, X-rayed me, and then afterwards bandaged it, and they said, 'Look, private, we're going to leave the piece in you. It's gone underneath a muscle and we'd have to cut the muscle and you'd have a big hole there. Now, we don't think that's going to do any harm. It's cauterised itself as it's gone in. I'm sure there won't be any infection there. In my opinion, it'd be best left in there.' And I've still got it.

Reg was away from his unit for six weeks.

When you rejoined the battalion, where were they?
Cassino still was going. We went to a little place way up in the rocky hills of Mt Cairo and we looked way down on the Liri Valley, which was the same sort of view that the monastery had. On 11 May the Poles and the British and all attacked Cassino while we were way up on the hill. We did a sort of sham attack — use your radio with false messages to create a bit of a diversion — but we weren't involved. We just watched the fireworks display from way up on the hill.

And from there we went to Sora. Sora's a very nice place, a lovely little town. We went through Sora. We had the Maoris up in the hills on our left and 21 Battalion was on the other side of the river, advancing with us. We were in a big valley, with hills each side of us.

We were on a little country lane. I was the sig to go with Major Aked, who was the second in command of the battalion. He had about five or six of us, with the jeep. We were going to run some lines to the platoons because they were going to be stationary, but then they decided not to do that. [There was] what I call a dog box, a railway station. It was just a small room with another floor on top of it, almost like a signal box of some sort. The commander was directing proceedings for the two companies up forward — they were about four or five hundred yards ahead of us. There was a big tree outside, on the side of the road. [Major Aked] said, 'Look at those cherries up there.' I said, 'I'll go and get some, sir.' So I got my haversack and emptied my things out — just my towel and soap and shaver — and I climbed up it. I was there for about three or four minutes, putting the cherries in this haversack, and next minute there was a big scream, and over came some shells. They burst all around us. The shrapnel was going through the trees and cherries were falling off. I tried to mould myself in amongst the tree. It all happened so quickly. Major Aked yelled out, 'Are you all right?' I said, 'Yes, I'm all right, sir.' So I brought the cherries down and we had a feed of cherries.

We carried on there and went right up to Avezzano. That was the only atrocity I saw. Twenty-two civilians were shot, all had been shot in a bomb hole and left there.

Do you know why that happened?

Something to do with partisan things, sabotage and that sort of thing. I saw seven kids there. There were two or three men, all the rest were women or children. [The Germans had been gone] about two or three hours. I just saw it, then we left. I think some British unit was coming up to take over. We were going back to another place.

We must have gone to a rest area called Arce then, after Avezzano. It would have been June, July 1944. I was then attached to A Company. We went to San Michele. Just before San Michele was a little town, about three or four miles south. We were going up to take a ridge of hills. Slow landscape going up to the hills.

There were two or three country lanes mixed in with little houses and villages going up to this place. A Company went into this big farmhouse complex. It was a three-storey stone building with outbuildings. We caught the Germans a bit by surprise, I don't know why. We got about 22 prisoners. It was quite easy. We also captured a German truck, so they put the prisoners in the German truck and one of our guys drove the truck back to Battalion Headquarters with the prisoners.

We'd been in this building for about two hours. On the right was 26 Battalion, and they'd advanced further up another country road towards the hills, another four or five hundred yards further up to another farmhouse. About two hours after we'd taken the prisoners and consolidated in this building, all hell broke loose, because obviously the Germans didn't appreciate this house being taken for tactical reasons, so he shelled us very heavily for half an hour. Then he shelled other areas to the extent that 26 Battalion lost both their tanks. There were no casualties, but it disabled the tanks. The whole area was plastered for several hours. 26 Battalion had to withdraw to behind us, and the tankie crew all scrambled into our building. One of them brought their Browning machine gun off the tank, plus ammunition. The shelling stopped for a while and then another big lot came in, and then we were counterattacked by a German regiment or something.

They encircled us. We were surrounded in the finish and we called what they call a 'murder', which is a heavy artillery stonk, on our own position. It worked too, although we got a couple of direct hits on the building. It was a very solid building — must have been there for hundreds of years. The Germans got a lot of casualties.

Sergeant Barrow and I had the back windows, we defended the back. We had the American Browning from the tanks. Oh, I forgot, during all this we had a heavy machine-gun section attached to us. The shelling got so heavy for them that they had to come inside, too, for protection. So we were quite an armed building. We had the tank, with their Browning machine gun, we had a Vickers machine gun, plus all our own arms plus, if we ran out of ammunition, we had a whole truckload of German ammunition in the barn down below.

That's the only time I thought I might be POW, but I only thought it for about half an hour and then I could see we were right. By that time D Company of our battalion had occupied the little village of San Michele, and [the Germans] attacked them. He had a Panther tank there. Our view was perfect because we were on a slight knoll of a hill, then it had a slight valley and up the other [side] was the village, so we looked straight across at them. The company commander, Major Howden, had all the guns pointing at San Michele in support of D Company, because D Company was then being counterattacked. They had a tank against them as well, which we didn't. It was funny because the tank, the Panther, came down this road with, I should say, half a dozen Germans sitting on the back of it. They soon went when the Browning opened up on them! I'm sure they must have killed a few of them off that tank, because it was really direct fire onto it.

Anyhow, we supported them as much as we could. They thought they'd have to retire too, but they held on and in the finish it was the air force — oh, I forgot to mention that while we were in dire straits, we had direct contact with the air force. We had an artillery O Pip with us when we got into this house, so we were very fortunate because that's how we brought the stonk on ourselves. The artillery O Pip also brought the air force on, and they strafed all around us. We sent a green and orange flare up and that identified our position, and then the DAF, Desert Air Force — it kept its name over in Italy — strafed all around us.

After about three or four days one intelligence officer went from our battalion and he counted over 107 bodies. So they had a lot of casualties, the Germans. In our little possie, we lost eleven killed, but more wounded.

After the excitement near San Michele, Reg went on to Empoli and then Siena, where he caught jaundice (hepatitis). He went to 2 New Zealand General Hospital at Caserta again for treatment, and rejoined the battalion on the east coast of Italy north of Rimini.

I asked to go back to A Company. We relieved the Canadians for a while. It was very wet. There was mud everywhere. The tanks could hardly move. It was a bit of a grind up there. Then we did a small attack across the Pisciatello River. It was too much for a tank to wade through, but it wasn't very big.

It was just a normal night attack. We had the searchlights acting as artificial moonlight and it worked very well too. [They shone them up] onto the clouds and the reflection came down, just like a nice moonlit night. I suppose we were about 200 yards behind our leading platoon, maybe a bit further. Everything was going all right for them and we were following our Bofors, which was firing our line of advance. We kept looking up as the tracer went over, and all of a sudden a shell landed very close to us. We were following a creeping barrage. It was pretty noisy. The platoon was keeping in close contact with the barrage, and we were a bit further behind it. This shell landed fairly close, then a few seconds later another shell landed close. The company commander realised that one of our guns was firing short, so we sent a message to Battalion [Headquarters], not that you could do much about it. [Then] he said, 'Right, let's double up, and we'll run up and get closer to the platoons. Get out of the range of this gun,' and there was an almighty crash. I had my big earphones with muffs over my ears so I didn't hear the explosion. I just saw it and felt it and landed on my face. My radio went dead. I took my earphones off and said to my other sig, 'What the hell happened there?' He said, 'One of the shells landed amongst us.' I said, 'My wireless is dead. Have a look, Bob.' He had his wee torch and he said, 'Half your set's missing.' I said, 'Come on. Let's get out of here.' So we did.

We had seven casualties. Nothing fatal, but a few what we call 'homers'. One of my personal friends, he lost most of his left hand, but he's all right.

It was a good attack too — that spoilt it — because we got quite a few prisoners. We got the sergeant major, the officer, their Don R with his motorbike and a big radio. So we had quite a good night, apart from that. It was a good haul. We got to a nice little house, amongst a lot of trees. Obviously it was the headquarters of this regiment, but they were a bit slow getting away. The rest of their troops had gone, but they were too slow. We were there for 24 hours, and our signal officer at that time was Ray Puck. He came up and brought me a new set and said to me, 'If that's what you're going to do with your radio, you're not going to get any more.'

The next day we advanced. And we stayed there for the

day. We got a fairly heavy shelling there that day. The battalion was then sent out of the lines to a rest area.

The radio that you had on your back, how much did it weigh?

It was quite heavy. It was in two sections — the top was the receiver, the bottom was the transmitter — and it had big joining connection wires. The battery sat in a compartment of its own underneath. On the outside you had a free aerial socket, so that if you went under a fence, it would bend and come back again.

We came back to the rest area, and then there was a real scramble and away we went — I'm talking about our whole battalion — up to Forli. Through Forli, up to the southern side of the Lamone River. On the other side was Faenza, the town of Faenza.

There was quite a bit of fighting, some skirmishes. We were in a holding position for a while. 22 Battalion did an attack, a sort of a pincer movement round Faenza. They had quite a few casualties. And then we got mostly round Faenza — in fact, we encircled it in the finish — not only us but other battalions.

The battalion — three of its companies (I think D was left in reserve) — got as far as the railway line. The railway line was on a bank about ten feet above ground level in this particular area. We got into a big house just this side of the railway line. There was a small country road running up towards a lot of farmhouses on the flat, and we had to do an attack that night to take two or three houses, and our other companies on our left were doing the same.

It was a silent attack. Just before I got there, one of our

platoons got caught badly in mines. I had to call the battalion for some ambulances. We left this house, climbed up over the railway line and went up towards these buildings. I suppose the first lot was about a thousand yards away.

Everything went quite well. The platoon got to the first house, but there was nothing there. It went to another small house, about 50, 60 yards ahead. Nothing. Major Howden made [the first house] our Company Headquarters, and about another four or five hundred yards further up, a platoon took a house, and took a couple of prisoners. Then, out of the blue, the Germans brought a tank in and our guys had to get out quickly. Our tanks couldn't get through because where the road went underneath the railway line [the Germans had] blown it and mined it, so they had to get the engineers to clear all the mines before our tanks could help us. It would be about twelve hours before that happened.

So, next thing we knew, Jack Price came back — he was the second lieutenant of 7 Platoon — and said, 'We've been driven out, sir. We've left four or five guys up there, wounded. We couldn't bring them out.' Major Howden said, 'We've got nothing here to fight the tanks, so we'd better get out.' So we had to go too.

They were attacked by German mortar fire as they retreated.

One of our medical guys stayed up there with our guys. Our other medic said to Major Howden, 'Sir, I think I'd better go up and help the guys.' Howden said, 'You know you'll be POW.' He said, 'Oh well. I have to go and see if they're all right.' So he went up too. He was taken prisoner. He got the MM for that. Evidently two or three guys were badly hurt.

By this time Faenza had been cleared, [and] we were back in Faenza. It was getting towards Christmas and we had occupied the outside of the bank [of the Senio River]. There were pockets of Germans still this side, here and there. We'd go into the line, take over from another battalion for a couple of weeks, then we'd go back.

> *After some time at Faenza the battalion was taken out of the line till March 1945. Reg was posted back to Battalion Headquarters in time for the last push over the Senio River and the fast pursuit of the Germans northwards.*

After we'd gone over two rivers pretty quickly, they made a [mobile] radio station and put me as the sig of it. First of all they put us in a Bren carrier. There were four of us as roving control. We were advancing so quickly, it was a good idea. We used to try and be close to the leading companies, and if Battalion couldn't hear them on the radio, we'd hear them because we were closer and we'd transfer the message. And vice versa. It worked quite well. Although one day we got a bit too keen — it was probably my fault, really. We were in a little country place and were advancing quite well. There was a double-storeyed house all on its own, and as we came round the corner of a hedge, I looked over and in a big ditch I saw a German bazooka. They must have just gone. We just got round the corner in the Bren carrier and a machine gun opened up at us. If a gun is firing at you, it's just like the crack of a whip.

If it's past, it's like a bang, but if it's straight towards you it's just a crack. It hit the carrier and I said, 'Let's back round the corner again.' So we backed round the corner out of sight of this building. I hopped out and went along the ditch to see. I saw four German steel helmets running down the hill, escaping, and we saw troops way over the back of us, coming over the paddocks. I had my field glasses and I put them on and I said, 'Christ, we're ahead of everybody.'

From there on we went head over heels all the time — it was just holdups through bridges and things like that. I know on the Adige River bridge, [there was] a real slaughter. The Germans had been going over the bridge and our air force must have caught them with rockets and strafing. God, the bodies were a mess. We had a Graves Unit, but sometimes it couldn't be done quickly. They probably lay there a week or so, sometimes more.

Cassino stunk. Oh, hell yes. Because they'd also been hit by bombs weeks and weeks before, and they probably hadn't been able to get the bodies out because the buildings had collapsed on them. We went into a building that [first] night and it stunk, because obviously it had happened two or three weeks ago. But it's funny how you got used to it, even as young as I was.

Were there people who did react really badly, though?
I just had one. Just before we started off from this house where the railway line was, [the Germans] gave us a real stonking over with nebelwerfers. I will agree that they're pretty nerve-wracking. They scream, a piercing scream, and then a crash, because it's all explosive and not much else. He went berserk.

I'd hardly known him — in fact, I still don't know how long he'd been with the battalion or where he came from. He only came to us about three hours before we started. He wouldn't move out of the place. He was scared stiff, absolutely terrified.

The battalion continued northwards.

They didn't need the roving control for the last couple of weeks before the war finished, and I just stayed with Battalion Headquarters until we got to Trieste. Our battalion went up into the hills. There were three little villages, all in a lateral road that ran into Trieste from the top. We could look way down onto Trieste, the harbour and everywhere. We stayed in Santa Croce for many months. There was tension there. The Yugoslavs, the partisans or Tito, wanted to reclaim Trieste. The Allies said no, and there was a bit of tension for a while.

Did you come across them yourself?
Oh yes, a lot of partisans. Half Santa Croce was full of partisans. They were quite friendly, up to a point. Not as friendly as the Italians were. They tolerated us, with a sort of reserved coolness.

We never left there till about October. Guys were going home all the time, and they told us that we didn't have a hope of getting home before Christmas because of the shipping. Guys that hadn't been over there very long were recruited for Jayforce in Japan. They were drafted out of our battalion — other battalions as well — and went to Florence to special barracks down there somewhere for training. And then we went down to Florence eventually. It was a sort of a rest camp, called 54 Rest Camp.

I left Taranto — when? Early January, because I'm pretty sure I landed back in New Zealand at the beginning of February 1946. My father and mother were there, and a couple of friends of mine.

What was it like being back?
Nothing seemed to have changed much, really. Mind you, it's a long time ago — I was probably thrilled to bits, I suppose. Apprehensive probably — what do I do now?

> *Reg settled back into civilian life, but joined the Regular Army in 1951 and served for twelve years. He and his wife, Dawn, lived in Auckland's eastern suburbs. Reflecting on his time in the army during the war, Reg has no regrets.*

We enjoyed it. It was a real adventure for us. I wouldn't have missed it for quids. Even now, I'm pleased that I went. I was lucky, you see. I'm all right.

'WE WERE ADVANCING BY STEPS'

RAE FAMILTON, 35882, MAJOR E.D., 20 AND 18 ARMOURED REGIMENTS

Rae Familton was born on 28 August 1913 in Hampden, North Otago, the seventh son in a family of eight. He spent his childhood in Oamaru, where he attended Oamaru North Primary School and Waitaki Boys' Intermediate and High Schools. He remembers his town's procession to mark the end of the First World War.

I'D JUST STARTED SCHOOL, AND I was a proud little bloke because I was put in the last seat in the wagon carrying the infants, with instructions to look after the rest. The other memory is of my brother travelling on a mock-up of a tank. He fell off and broke his arm.

My father was a plumber, and was born in New Zealand. My mother came from Falkirk, Scotland. She was a strong Methodist, and sang in the choir. My father was in the 5 Otago Mounted Rifles Hussars brass band. In those days of Saturday-morning work, one of the highlights for the week was that either my father or one of my older brothers would bring home the latest record — opera, chamber music, a singer or a brass band. After lunch on Saturdays we'd go to the sitting room and listen to the latest record. I was brought up in a musical family and I appreciate music still.

After he left school Rae attended both Dunedin and Auckland Teachers' Colleges. He did not rush to enlist when war was declared in September 1939.

I was courting at the time. We were more or less engaged. Things crop up in your mind, and you sit down and think about it. I decided two things. One, I would complete my training and get myself a permanent job to return to. Two, I wouldn't marry, because I might be killed. I finished my year in Auckland, came back to Dunedin and taught the first term at Caversham School as a physical education specialist. I got a permanent job at Central School, Palmerston North, put in one term and then joined the army. I went into Trentham Camp. What a hilarious trip that was. We all arrived — there must have been four or five hundred men — with our ties cut off at the knot. A group [had] gone through the train with scissors and cut off everybody's ties. We all marched off the train with just the knot in our ties.

Rae went overseas in 1942 and was posted to B Squadron of 20 Armoured Regiment. He remembers the action at Cassino.

We moved up to a place called Mignano. It was just bare paddocks with trees, and about six miles south of Cassino. We were to take over from the Yanks and go into action at Cassino. We were all on edge preparing for this great attack. We had a look at Cassino from the top of Mt Trocchio. It didn't look very healthy at all, with the monastery sitting at the top there, looking down on everything. It gave absolute observation of everything we did. Now, we were military and if we'd been there, we would have used it for observation. Definitely. We were certain the Germans used it for observation, absolutely certain.

Then the whole show was delayed for some reason. We were all prepared to go, and everything was stopped for six days. You can imagine the tension and then the letdown, so the squadron commander decided that we must get some plonk and relax. We relaxed with a great little party, and then settled down in dirty, rotten, wet, cold weather under some olive trees, waiting for the next attack on Cassino.

Did you see the bombing of the monastery?

Yes, I did. Six hundred planes. Waves of them coming over. It was a beautiful day and you could see the detonations travelling through the air.

There was a little dam on the Rapido River. They blew the dam, and flooded the Rapido Valley. It made it awkward. The only track in after the bombing was the railway line, strangely enough. Tanks went across the railway line to support our blokes.

I was in and out myself. I was battle captain of the squadron, taking up supplies, so I wasn't in the actual battle within the confines of Cassino itself, but I saw it from outside.

One of the interesting things about Cassino was that the Americans had what they called a T2, a Sherman tank with the turret taken off and sheer legs mounted as a crane. They used it to recover knocked-out tanks. We didn't have one. The

Americans walked off and left one bogged in the Rapido River in front of Cassino, so our squadron flying fitters, Charles Lilley, Jack Dever, Harry Amman and George Taylor, went in every night and recovered this thing. They had to replace a track and check the engine, and all the rest of it, and every time they hit the track with a sledgehammer, you know what happened: down came the mortars. They'd have a couple of smacks at the track, and then dive into the turret or under the tank until the mortars stopped. They went in for about six nights and finally recovered the T2. And there we were, we had a recovery tank in 20 Regiment. 'Whisky Bill' [Inglis] was tickled pink about this until he was informed by the general that the Americans heard we had a T2 and charged us £30,000 for its purchase.

One of the tragedies of war [happened] in Cassino. A Balclutha family had already lost two sons in the desert. The third son, Vince, was in the squadron with us. We took him out of the tank and placed him driving trucks in the B Echelon. We lost a driver at Cassino, and it was Vince's old tank. He came to me and said, 'I'm going up to my old crew.' I said, 'That will be the day, Vince. You've lost two brothers. You're staying with your truck.' He said, 'No bloody show, I'm going back with the boys. That's where I belong and that's who I've been with, and I'm going.' I said, 'I can't send you. I'm thinking of your family.' He said, 'I'm thinking of my family. I'm thinking of my brothers too.' We didn't have anybody trained as a driver, so in the finish I had to send him up. Killed. Three sons.

An officer's life is not always a happy one when you've got to do things like that.

We struck a new German gun there. We think it was 170-millimetre. It was mounted on a railway truck, and they kept it in the tunnel on the railway about half a mile behind Cassino. They would bring this truck out of the tunnel, line her up, and all of a sudden there would be a bloody great explosion in amongst you. Then you'd hear the bang. They'd fire three rounds and go back into the tunnel. The air force couldn't spot it, we couldn't spot it. It wasn't until the final fall of Cassino we found [where] they had this damned gun. It was a frightening thing, because you got the explosion first and the bang of the gun afterwards. The shell travelled faster than the speed of sound.

Then we were withdrawn, and the Poles came in for the final attack on the monastery. My job was to take half the squadron and go round and capture the German headquarters at a place called Sora, behind Monte Cassino. I got quite poetical about the red poppies and the green grass and the fruit trees in the valleys as we came over. I suppose after the mud and the blood and the snow and the rain and the dirt and the filth of Cassino for thirteen weeks, it was a magnificent view from the top of the pass. We got down into the valley and Sora was about four miles ahead of us. This beautiful valley hadn't been touched. 19 Regiment were going to the right and I was going to the left, and all of a sudden shells and God knows what went flying everywhere. Up came Brigadier Keith Stewart in a tank. He stopped beside my tank, and suddenly a truck brewed up ahead of us and a truck brewed up behind us and we were in the middle. Who brewed them up? The Royal Air Force. Keith Stewart somehow saw a number on the plane and reported it to the air force. That poor pilot was grounded for 24 hours for bombing short and bombing a New Zealand brigadier.

The Balsorano Valley from Sora pointed due north with high hills on either side, and the Jerry artillery was sitting up there. The only way we could advance was along the bottom. As the attack went up the valley we were relieved by 18 or 19 Regiment. We settled in for a rest, and I went for my rounds about nine o'clock at night to see if everybody was settled in. The wine had been flowing a bit. I called in at the flying fitters' tent. They had a supply of wine. I'd had a few wines, but not many, and they insisted that I sit down and have a couple with them. A couple became a couple more. We were right in the middle of a stubble field, and when I decided it was time I got the hell out of it and got home to my bed they held me down and pinched my boots. I had to walk home through these fields in my stockinged feet. Could you imagine that happening in the British Army? You couldn't.

We were pulled out of the line then and went for a rest. Then we were brought back in. A town had been attacked and taken the day before, and we were going to relieve both the infantry and the armour the next morning. We got into the town. It was a great little town, but very badly bombed and knocked about in the attack. Trying to go through the town we came to a demolition in the road. As we had orders to move and keep pushing at the Germans, I had to find a way for my tanks to get through with the infantry. I looked along the street, and here was a right of way between two two-storey houses which met above. I measured my tank with my eye and [thought], I might be able to do it, so I said to my driver, 'We'll shut down everything, turret and all, and I'll walk in front and guide you. We'll go through that right of way and beat the demolition.' I got the tank, I would think, halfway through the right of way when the driver must have pulled the wrong lever, because he swung around about six inches. That hit the wall of one house, and the whole two top floors came down on top of the tank. I had to get the other two tanks of the troop to hook on the rear and pull it back again. We didn't get through until the engineers had the demolition cleared and partly filled. The trials and tribulations.

We had a fellow who was an old gold miner from Central Otago. He was our sanitary corporal, an explosives expert. After Sora I said to him, 'You've got to do something about these flies, especially round the cookhouse. They're a damned nuisance and they're a health risk.' He went away and set his mind to work, and then one of the boys said to me, 'You'd better get down to the cook shop and see Dave's latest experiment.' I went down and there was Dave. He'd got a sheet of tin about two foot square, the edges turned up, fine copper wires squared across it and some raspberry jam on the base of it. He was sitting there, drinking a mug of tea, and every time flies settled he connected up his twelve-volt battery and cleaned up that lot. Then he went on with his mug of tea — then bang went another lot of flies.

In June 1944, the division trained and rested in Arce before continuing on towards Florence.

We were on the left and our friends the South Africans were on the right. This is a sore point with a lot of New Zealand soldiers — every morning when the American paper came out and the news came on the BBC, the South Africans were advancing towards Florence. The *real* story was that the New Zealand Division did night attacks and then the South Africans came up in the morning. But it was their turn for publicity, we think. I'll never forget 'Whisky Bill' Inglis after a few vinos one night saying, 'These South Africans, they don't like attacking in daylight and they never bloody well attack at night, but we'll get on to the job.'

I went with a half squadron with the Maori Battalion, and it was pretty hot fighting for three or four days on the way up there. We were advancing steadily and Jerry was pulling back. He had a line behind the Arno River, so he was just pulling back and holding as much as he could, getting back by steps. We were advancing by steps. I think we did about three night attacks in a row there. We got to the bank of the Arno, and I was just 150 yards to the east of the Ponte Vecchio bridge and Jerry was sitting on the other side of the river. He saw us moving and we saw him moving, but Florence had fallen so no shots were fired. I said to one of the troop commanders, 'I wonder if there's any way across the Arno here?' He calmly walked down and along the bank of the river. Nobody fired and Merv Cross had a good look and said, 'There's no hope of crossing here.'

Rae reflects on the effect of being in action.

We had one driver whose tank was hit, and he was wounded and sent to the rear. The wound was in his big toe and they chopped it off. With penicillin, he was back with us in ten days. I said to him, 'You'd better drive a truck for a while.' He said, 'It's only a bloody toe, I've come back to drive my tank with the boys. I've been with them all the way and I'm going to stay with them.' I put him back in his tank and went on up to the start line for the next action. The barrage opened and his tank didn't move, so I called out. His tank commander called out that this driver had freaked out. He was quite happy to be back into action, he said there was nothing wrong with him, and yet as soon as the shellfire started from the barrage, he just went to pot. We had to pull him out of his seat and hustle in another driver and get on the way. He was sent home, quite rightly, I think. He wasn't a coward. It was just that his nervous system couldn't take the effects of being hit in his tank. It was a totally different attitude from what it was in World War One. A bloke like that would have been shot in World War One for cowardice. We had enough nous and we'd heard enough that if anything like that happened, it was handed straight over to the medical people.

Occasionally you'd get the fellow who shot himself in the foot — SIW, self-inflicted wound — but very, very seldom. The Kiwis that I knew and served with were good soldiers, damned good soldiers. In a tank unit you were a tight-knit team, five in each tank, a crew. You were with your cobbers and you all worked in together. I think that might have had a better influence on how fellows felt. You were never alone. So [easy to be] afraid when you're alone.

After Florence, the fighting that the New Zealand Division was involved in moved to the other side of Italy.

The Germans were pulling back towards their fortified lines at Rimini to try and stop us breaking out into the Po Valley. General [Freyberg] decided that the tanks would attack without infantry to try and keep contact with the Jerry. We called it the Gambettola Savio Gallop. On the first day they used self-propelled guns mounted on tank chassis against us. On the start line that morning one of the boys said to me, 'You and I have been in every ruddy action in Italy. One of us is going to collect it, Rae.' I thought, Don't talk bloody rot. Nobody knows that. We came to one of these sunken country roads. The tanks went down one side and up the other and we got to slow down. The two forward tanks were going across when a self-propelled gun appeared on the left, about 500 yards up the road, and let one go. It went between the head of the driver and the gun in my tank. The driver felt the heat of it going past. It hit the bloke who had said to me, 'One of us is going to get it today' in the next tank, and took his leg off. Premonition? I don't know.

We settled in. The infantry came up round the tanks to protect us at night. I went to the orders group [meeting] and was ordered to get a crossroads which would be quite vital to supply in reinforcement the next morning. It was about a mile ahead of where we were. I only had two troops, a half squadron. Two troops and my headquarters tanks. I did what I considered a perfect tactical advance. At first light of morning, one troop went up, covered by the other troop. I only had one troop commander. The other troop was commanded by the sergeant major, and the two reserve troops were commanded by sergeants — we were that far down on officers at that stage. When Phil Crespin, the troop commander, arrived at the crossroads he saw a jeep sitting there. He pulled up to the jeep and a very distinctive voice said to him, 'Good morning. Where are you going?' Here was General Freyberg having a look himself. He certainly kept up with the battle wherever he possibly could in Egypt and Italy, and he knew what was going on.

We advanced a little further that day, and then were pulled out to prepare for the advance through Rimini into the Po Valley. That night the colonel called me in and said, 'You're going into action again tomorrow because we've had an international incident. Our friends, the Greeks, have appealed to their friend, General Freyberg, and have said that the Canadians have not given them any support with armour and artillery in any way, and they have been pushed a little back off their objective. They want to take it back again and they'd like New Zealand to support them on it. So General Freyberg has ordered that we send them a half squadron of Shermans to help the Greeks.' I reported to the Greek headquarters, and there were flowery speeches about the wonderful friendship between the Greeks and New Zealanders. We all shook hands and everybody was happy.

Jack Shacklock, who had been our Technical Officer, was going into action for the first time as a troop fighter. We advanced at first light with the Greek infantry. Ahead was a big clump of high bamboo. There was noise in the bamboo, and movement. Jack couldn't see what it was, so he let go with a great burst of machine-gun fire. We've never let him forget it. Out came a rooster and six hens.

We pushed forward. At first light we'd got on the Greeks' original objective, and at five o'clock in the morning I had a deputation from their colonel and several senior officers again thanking me for the assistance from our great friends the New Zealanders. We finished up putting them on their line ready for the advance on Rimini airfield, which was about four miles away at that stage. This was probably the luckiest day of my life in the war, because 18 Regiment took over and travelled that four miles with the Greeks. They got to the edge of the airfield and the Germans had dug in three turrets with 88-millimetre guns. The Eighteenth suffered mighty casualties — tanks knocked out, killed and wounded.

The New Zealand Division continued on its way through the Po Valley.

The breakout was made and the push was on towards Forli. I was returning from a reconnaissance with another officer when all of a sudden a battery of nebelwerfers opened up. The roads were built up in the Po Valley, above the level of the river flooding, so we got on the side of the road away from the Germans and [these] amazing fireworks came from the glare of these nebelwerfer batteries firing at us. We counted thirteen shells, which landed on the far side of the road. Not one exploded. We were told afterwards by the Engineers that those shells were all filled with sand. They were all made in [German-occupied] Czechoslovakia. We are very thankful to the Czechoslovaks.

We found the going pretty difficult in the Po Valley. It was winter. The rivers and ditches and tarsealed roads became icy in the mornings with frost. [The weather] settled in by the time we got to Faenza, and we became stuck for the rest of the winter. There we were joined by a series of searchlight batteries supplied by the British forces. The searchlights were set up so many hundred yards behind us, and their lights were focused on the clouds just above the German lines. The theory was that it would blind the [Germans] and make seeing things quite difficult. Apparently it did so. These searchlight batteries were commanded by one British major. I don't know how I met him, but I invited him to come and have a drink with us at our little mess. I'd taken over the top floor of quite a biggish house at Forli. The householders were a bit worried because their daughter was getting married, and that was supposed to be the place where the marriage was carried out. I said, 'Don't worry. You hold your wedding there and we'll clean all our stuff out, then put it back after the wedding's over.' I received an invitation to be present at the wedding — quite a to-do for the family, almost in the front line of a war.

There was a distillery [in Forli]. It made great wine. Vermouth. It was strange that most of the water carts in the regiment didn't carry water for the first week we were there, they carried vermouth. They had to put a stop to that, because you have water for a lot of other things besides drinking.

On New Year's Eve, the Maoris were playing two-up in the town square and all of a sudden there was that droning noise of the three-engined German bomber. Dead on midnight, it dropped one bomb and went home again, just to say, 'Welcome in the New Year'. The Maoris weren't very pleased, because they lost a bit of money in their two-up school.

At that stage we weren't striking many German fighter aircraft because they had all been taken away for other fronts in Europe. I think poor old [German commander, Field Marshal Albert] Kesselring was left with a lot of infantry and not a great deal of support for them.

Rae was then sent to Maadi Camp in Egypt to pick up the troops in the Sixteenth Reinforcements, but as they were not needed because the war was

*ending, he was soon ordered back to his regiment
in Italy.*

I contacted RAF base headquarters and got onto a Halifax
bomber and we flew back through the Greek islands, through
Cos and Rhodes, on to Italy. The poverty and filth in some of
those Greek places where the Jerries had absolutely devastated
the areas. What rocked us was to see the eleven- and twelve-
year-old girls offering you sex for one piece of bread. They
were absolutely starving. It was a really depressing sight. I got
back to Bari, handed in my papers and was told to catch a flight
up to the front, just short of Trieste.

We got up to Trieste and I was billeted in one of the big
pubs on the waterfront. We had A squadron at the seaplane
base at the head of the bay and B squadron, to which I was
attached, along the waterfront. There were tanks in the town
square, opposite the government offices. This was only about
five or six days after Trieste was taken.

I was taken out to see what was going on, and what amazed
me was to see a Yugoslav patrol coming along through one of
the side roads. Here were six Yugoslavs, [looking] a bit weedy,
laden down with arms. But who was the sergeant in charge? A
girl with [a] Sten gun under her arm, a pistol on one hip and
two grenades hanging on the other one. The men told me they
would be shot at dawn if they made her pregnant.

The [Yugoslavs] tried to force their way into Trieste. They
had armoured patrols right up to the city. They tried to take
the city over before we did, and were only forced to fall back
because we put tanks in the front line with troops aboard and
guns pointing at them. I was very sympathetic to the Italians,

because I felt that Trieste was really a part of Italy. I don't think the Yugoslavs had either a cultural or a political claim on the city itself. I think it was a move by the Communists to enlarge Yugoslavia and get the good port. [The] Yugoslavs were pretty harsh to the Italian population, and it wasn't until we forced them out of the city itself that the Italian people really settled down and started to return to normal. The situation was pretty tense for about ten days and then seemed to calm down. There was a feeling that we might have to fight the Yugoslavs, and I think the division would have stayed if that had happened. We were still part of the Eighth Army in Italy, and if the army had had to fight we'd have had to fight.

What about after the hostilities had ceased?
We got on very well with the Italian people. We were treated as victors and as liberators. We had flowers given to us and, of course, plenty of vino. The morale of the division was good. We went on leave to Florence, and into Venice. My old troop was into Venice very early because General Freyberg wanted the Hotel Danieli, where he'd spent his honeymoon, as the leave centre for New Zealand troops. My old troop took members of 22 Motor Battalion aboard the tanks and trundled into Venice and took the hotel over.

Was there any thought that you might now be heading off towards the Pacific?
Yes, because we knew that our government had decided that we would have to have some input into the Pacific. There was a great deal of uncertainty. I got back to the regiment and there'd been a few casualties and a few furloughed blokes, so

the promotions came through and I got my majority and was transferred to 18 Armoured Regiment to take over the squadron left by Major Alan Pyatt, who went to England to train in the ministry and became Bishop of Christchurch.

It seemed to us that we might be in the hot seat if anything was required for Japan. We weren't very happy, because I don't think any of us wanted to go to jungle warfare after the open warfare of [North Africa] and the reasonably open warfare in Italy. I'd been six years in the army at that stage, although my active service was only in the Italian campaign. I was very much of the opinion that I got the hell out of it and got on with my life, because life was slipping away. I was 32, not a chicken.

The adjutant of 18 Regiment, myself and my driver batman decided to have a bit of leave and go for a trip round north Italy. The colonel said, 'You needn't come back unless you've got some beer.' He told me that he knew of a brewery some-where in the Po Valley, and we were to bring home a supply of beer. I can't remember the name of the place; however, we found it. We pulled in and I went into the office, and rapped on the glass panel. I said, 'I believe I can get some beer here.' A young lady's voice said, 'Another bloody Kiwi.' I put my head through and there was a very nice-looking young lady. I said, 'Where do you come from?' She said, 'From Australia, but I've been in New Zealand. I came home in 1939 to visit my grandparents and I've been here ever since.' We got a very good supply of beer at a very reasonable price and headed off home to Trieste.

Rae remembers the importance of keeping in touch with people at home.

We all used to write pretty regularly. Every week, except when you were in action. When you were going into action you immediately wrote a letter home just in case anything happened. In Maadi Camp we had some idea when we were getting mail, because when the flying boat came in and landed on the Nile we knew that air-letter cards had arrived from New Zealand. Sometimes you'd go quite a long time before you got any letters, but it was a great day when news came from home — and great disappointment if you lined up the boys in your troop and one or two blokes got nothing. In the tanks they shared letters with those blokes. They read them out in parts. They were very good that way.

He also remembers having to censor mail.

You used to get your troop mail in once a week. You'd read it all through and cut out pieces which mentioned manoeuvres or anything like that. You had to read a lot of private matters between husbands and wives and families. In the main I think the Kiwis played the game, but occasionally you had to take a razor blade and cut a piece out of a letter.

I didn't see a New Zealand group during the war whose morale wasn't good, although I know that in Italy, towards the end, our infantry were getting very tired. I don't think they'd lost their morale, I think they were merely getting tired. We had plenty of leave. We made our own fun. We were not called 'Freyberg's circus' for nothing. We lived pretty well, and I think our morale on the whole was very, very good.

Rae came home on the Strathmore.

I can remember very little about it. The blokes were so happy at getting home that everything went pretty swimmingly. We struck one of those Great Australian Bight storms. I'm a good sailor, but when your ship's going up and down, and to the right and to the left in a corkscrew movement, it doesn't matter how good a sailor you are. However, we got home. We got to Wellington, unloaded, and went across in the ferry. The dirty rotten dogs, they put me in charge of the train to Invercargill: inspect the train when you board, inspect the train when you leave. But when I got to Dunedin I couldn't be bothered. I was off. I could see my wife there and I'd been away for a few years, so I left the inspection of the train to somebody else.

Rae had married in 1942. After the war he completed his BA in History at Otago University while teaching at Mornington Primary School, then Macandrew Intermediate. He then transferred to King's High School, where he remained for 23 years, retiring as deputy principal in 1976. He also continued his contact with things military. He commanded C Squadron, 1 Armoured Car Regiment, New Zealand Scottish in the early days of compulsory military training, and also commanded the King's High School cadet battalion for many years.

'YOU WERE CALLED PADRE'

Jack SOMERVILLE, 81229, Padre, Captain, 19 Armoured Regiment

Jack Somerville, one of the seven children of James and Grace Somerville, was born in Dunedin in 1910. He attended Otago Boys' High School and Otago University, from which he graduated in 1935 with an MA in English. He then trained for the ministry for three years at Knox College. In 1937–38 he attended Westminster, a Presbyterian theological college at Cambridge University. After returning to New Zealand in 1938, he was ordained in December and became a minister at Tapanui, near Gore.

THERE WAS NOT A GREAT deal of consciousness about war and its effects in those early 1930s, but Hitler gradually advanced on the scene and things changed. I went to Britain in 1937 for the first time as a student, and we weren't unduly alarmed about any sort of war at that stage. It came to a peak, of course, when the war started and I felt, after a time, that I had to do something about this, so I offered myself as a chaplain, in spite of the fact that I had strong misgivings about war itself.

It was a tussle. I didn't feel convinced enough that this

was the right course I should take, completely denying any participation in fighting of any kind. Even though I didn't bear arms, of course, I still was mixed up with the whole shooting match. There was a tension there, there's no doubt about it. I suppose I overcame it because I thought that that's where I should be. There were people who needed the gospel.

I was minister of the parish [in Tapanui] and I knew that the church had important interests in providing chaplains for the care — spiritual and otherwise — of the personnel in the army. I was a free agent. I wasn't married, I'd served for a while in this parish. I thought I should offer myself, whatever the consequences, and I did. I felt my main duty was not so much patriotic as a Christian duty. I had sympathy with New Zealand's role in the war, to preserve the world from whatever Hitlerism meant, but basically I felt that here were men and women offering themselves to serve their country, who needed some sort of basis for their lives, some sort of Christian understanding of what it was all about, if that was possible, and someone to be with them when they were facing death — everyone who went there faced death, there's no doubt about that. In any case, I was a free agent, so I offered.

In May 1941 Jack went into camp at Trentham.

I recall the sergeant major who whipped us around the parade ground. He was a terrible fellow, gave us hell. We had some study periods about the war, background to it and that sort of thing, but it was mainly drill. The military people were fairly sympathetic to the padres on the whole. They gave us a pretty good run.

I think you required the training to know what all the military stuff was about — the kind of language you would be using, the kind of people you were going to be meeting, the kind of way in which they organised their lives, and how you fitted into that. We had to learn that, but once you got into it, then you acted as an ordinary minister. We were living in a different sort of world, and that what's the training was really about. It wasn't marching up and down the parade ground (though that kept us fit, I suppose), but finding out how another sort of world operated.

I always wanted to do the best I could for the people I was serving. When you got into the army you were under some sort of discipline, even as a chaplain, even though you weren't a military person. You had to conform to the system of life in a camp. That was a bit irksome. You also had to make your own way to a large degree. You were accepted and then you were thrown into the deep end. You made contacts with the personnel. Some of them would be Christians of various kinds, and you'd probably get together with them — that was one thing we did — but my view was to be in touch as much as possible with all sorts of people, and that took a bit of doing. It was very different being minister in a parish and being a chaplain in a set-up which had a completely closed kind of format.

Jack had the rank of captain.

Sometimes it inhibited you, because you knew jolly well that a lot of the men thought that you were just another bloody officer. That was probably a bad thing. I don't know how you could have exercised your ministry without that kind of gradation, as it were. If you were just one of the men, as you probably ought to have been, you'd have to fit into a system which gave you no chance to operate, because the privileges of officer status allowed you to do the things that you thought you should do — organise things, run things.

Church services were of different kinds as time went on in the army. Originally, church parades were compulsory and everybody had to go. You took the service, and everybody sang either properly or a bowdlerised version of things, but they could be quite meaningful. There were two kinds — the Sunday parade, which was a proper church service, but short. We always had the good sense, I think, to cut them short. And the daily prayers. Every morning the regiment would be lined up and everybody put in order and paraded around, then the colonel would say 'Padre,' and I would step forward and say perhaps a short Bible reading and a prayer, and that was it. Finished. That was every day. Those things were part of the drill but for the Sunday services, you had to work very hard to keep their attention.

In March 1942 Jack was posted to the Second Tank Regiment at Waiouru.

The regiment was made up mainly of men from Wellington province. It was a bit of a shock to get the music of 'Sussex by the Sea' at six o'clock in the morning. To a certain degree it was enjoyable, because we were finding out what it was going to be like to be a chaplain. We slept in tents, so it had its rigours.

We were preparing to go overseas and join the 2NZEF in the

Middle East. At that stage the decision had been made to send one of the regiments overseas. The whole lot, of course, went in due course, but in stages. The first one to go was 3 Tank Regiment, 'Three Tanks' they were called. There was One Tanks, Two Tanks, Three Tanks. I was transferred to Pukekohe Camp preparatory to getting onto the ship and going to the Middle East. I transferred from Two Tanks to Three Tanks, and in many ways that was a pleasant enough change because I was with the South Island group. It was the Three Tanks lot which were part of the large number of personnel that went overseas on the *Aquitania* [in December 1942] and were known as the Eighth Reinforcements.

I recall the approach to Egypt through the Red Sea. We had one or two scares. We had to take a zigzag course because of reported enemy submarines, and we did this sort of thing for some miles. That was in the approaches to Port Said. I remember landing at Port Said and going to Maadi Camp, but not in detail. It was largely meeting people and getting posted to whatever it was I had to be posted to. And, of course, the heat.

Egypt was largely a camp experience. We were settled in Maadi Camp for a long time, I've forgotten how many months. It was quite a while, because we got there in the new year and we went to Italy later on in the year, in October [1943]. The division had fought the desert war, and people were coming back at that stage. Many of them were going back on leave to New Zealand, and others were being incorporated into the tank brigade. And that was a delicate operation, let me tell you. The old digs, the people who had fought in the desert, were uneasy, or perhaps sometimes even bolshie, towards the new recruits, the Eighth Reinforcements, who hadn't touched a weapon in anger. Even through the ranks of the officers, it was felt. It was something which didn't really go away until we were blooded. I think even in our reunions, over the years, you felt a touch sometimes that the old digs, the ones who were in the desert and went right up to Tripoli and came into the tank regiments, were just a little bit superior. They'd tasted the real war before the others had, lost friends, and that sort of thing.

Jack was posted to 19 Armoured Regiment.

I stayed there right through to peace, to the end of the war.

He sailed with the regiment for Italy.

It was a high-security effort that one, but we landed safely, fortunately. There was a bit of activity in the skies for the next week or so. Taranto was quite pleasant, with a certain amount of shelter, but not a great deal. [It was a] fairly open camp and it was bombed fairly regularly, but gradually everybody was gathering up to move on. We didn't stay in Taranto long. Then we moved on up the east coast of Italy, to Bari first, and by December we were thrown into action at Perano, which is near the Sangro River, where New Zealand tanks first struck the enemy. That was our first introduction to actual fighting.

Where were you during the battle?
Normally in battle situations I was with the Regimental Aid Post, which is the place where the wounded are first brought to, and from which people went out to bring wounded in. That was

the major pattern that I adopted. Myself and the batman driver could see and help people who were brought in wounded, or else we went out from there to bring people in or do what ever was necessary. And we were there at the Regimental Aid Post when people came in and required some sort of ministry. So that was the major role, the major ministry, that I exercised.

When everything was over, a chaplain would sometimes go back to a Casualty Clearing Station with people who were wounded or in trouble. And then, as the battle moved on, I had the job of burying those who could be found, and in tank warfare that's a much more tricky job. It's bad enough in any situation, but tank warfare was pretty grim as far as burying was concerned, because most of the casualties in tanks were *in* the tanks. Incinerated. It's not a very pleasant memory.

I had my first burials at the Sangro, at the battle of Perano, and I remember it vividly. The Italians are a volatile sort of people, emotionally volatile. They didn't know the boys that were killed and buried but they gathered around the graves and wept, which was their natural way of showing their feelings. We wouldn't have done that with people we didn't know. It was strange to us. I felt it was good that these people were willing to come out of their casas to where we were gathered. It was comforting.

Jack spent most of the rest of the winter of 1943-44 with the regiment at Orsogna.

People were very kind — if we wanted vino, we could have it until it ran out of our ears. There was an interest in knowing about our families, where we came from, what our country was like. They were very welcoming. With a good background of Latin, I found Italian words and phrases quite easy to pick up. Within a week or two it came quite easily. I didn't know Italian as such, but the background of Latin that there is in Italian was enough to give me a fair sense of the meaning, so that in ordinary conversation I gradually picked things up.

The New Zealand Division moved to the west of Italy in preparation for the battle of Cassino.

The approach to Cassino was interesting. Route 6 was the main road, which went up through Cassino, bore left out towards the coast and then on to Rome. On the right of Cassino township and Monte Cassino there were a lot of hills and rivers. They were quite difficult rivers to cross.

We did have action on the way into Cassino, but I don't think our unit shared in that very much. We had to come up and take up a position near Cassino. The area south of Cassino where we set up was honeycombed with little roads and farms and streams. It was fairly heavily populated with small farms. We went up and took up a position.

There were two phases, at least as far as I was concerned, with Cassino. The first was the initial attempt to do something in February 1944, which didn't come off very well. That was when massive bombing took place and the monastery at the top of Mount Cassino was pounded. There was some sort of attempt to deal with the town, but the main thrust at Cassino was in March.

I don't know whether it was a wise move or not. I supported the possible bombing of the monastery, because it was such a key position and I'm sure that it was used as an observation post and there were German troops in the basement, in the lower parts of the monastery.

Anyway, the monastery was bombed. Sometimes one wonders whether it was a fair thing to do. I don't think there was a great loss of life but, of course, there was the loss of what must have been a very treasured building. Most of the art treasures were preserved. They'd hidden them.

The bombing was a horrific experience to hear and to see. The noise. The problem left behind was that they'd destroyed every possible means of access to the monastery because the roads were shattered. It left great holes and floodwaters. There were a lot of lives lost because of that. Whether it was the right tactic or not, as far as actually taking Cassino, I don't know. It wasn't taken till May.

We were in the Regimental Aid Post, which was on Route 6 right under the mount, and could be seen quite well. It was quite a big Regimental Aid Post because it was a central one, and people came from every direction with wounded. I had my driver and we were called out from time to time to get people in. I remember going out in our jeep, the two of us, and taking the turn that took you onto Route 6, right underneath the hill. You could be seen completely. The junction with reinforcements and people like us going up to the front line was obvious, and how we got through that, I don't know. Turning the corner onto Route 6 is something I shan't forget.

Cassino was a strange experience. We were there in February, we were there in March. New Zealand people came out after the March battle, and most of them rested, but in May, when the final onslaught was undertaken, 19 Regiment were taken up and their tanks were used for a very short period. And then, of course, it was all over. So we had quite a time at Cassino.

I remember going with friends from the ground level, as it were, up the road and into the monastery and seeing the devastation immediately, more or less, after the Germans surrendered. It was a terrible tangle. Trees everywhere, torn about, dead, rocks and buildings strewn everywhere. All sorts of things buried in the mess. I managed to snaffle a book which is in the Knox College library now. It's in Greek and it's very old, I suppose about fourteenth century.

Following Cassino we went to Rome. I had leave, then we were engaged in the fighting north of Rome towards Florence, and we lost one or two of our good people in those battles. Later on, on the east coast again towards Rimini and up the Po Valley, we had some quite heavy fighting at some of the river crossings there. We spent the next Christmas at a place called Faenza. I remember that well, because it was heavily attacked and the place where we had our Christmas service was in the basement of an old house which had been knocked about. Then we went on to Trieste.

It was as a result of his activities during the action to cross the Gaiana River that Jack won a Military Cross. The official citation reads, 'On the 17th April 1945, in the action on Canale Gaiana, very heavy opposition was unexpectedly encountered. The Padre, on his own initiative immediately went forward to the advance elements and under extremely heavy mortar and machine gun fire, organised evacuation of wounded infantry and

tank personnel. His presence at this critical period of
the advance had an immediate effect on the morale
and determination of our troops and undoubtedly
influenced the stabilising of our position.'

I wouldn't have written it up in the terms in which they wrote
it up. I remember taking the stretcher and the stretcher-bearer
and my driver, and going down and finding people in trouble
and taking two or three of them out. It was nothing notable
apart from the fact that it was a bit tricky. Maybe they wanted
to find some kind of excuse for giving me the Military Cross, I
don't know. The sad thing about it was that one of the people
I admired very much, although I got him out, he died.

And then it was pretty straight going up to Trieste. The New
Zealanders thought that it was all over, more or less, but there
was tension in Trieste: the situation was that the Yugoslavs
wanted to get a toehold into western Europe. It took a bit of
diplomacy as well as a little bit of military flag-waving to stop
that.

How did you view the Yugoslav forces in Trieste?
Didn't view them very much at all. I don't remember them.
We didn't see much of them at all. We called them the 'Jugs',
that's all that I remember. But I think that the background of
the Russians was a more menacing element in the situation.
From my memory and my point of view, we were so pleased
to be in a situation where we could see it was all ending that
it would have been a very unfortunate and strange reversal to
have had to get involved in another scrap.

[The regiment] had a party to celebrate my Military Cross in

Trieste. I remember that. It sounds as if it was a bit of a holiday, but there was this tension in the background. We were waiting to break up and go home in due course. I think the division was in remarkably good shape. Morale was reasonable, and it was a much more civilised situation than we had been in for a while.

After the cessation of the hostilities, the biggest and most interesting experience I had was the chaplains' leadership school at Riccione on the east coast of Italy. During the waiting period to go home, the chaplains' department was entrusted with the job of running a leadership school [for the troops] to give some background to those that wanted it of what we were involved with when we got home, and also some teaching about the Christian faith. I and three others were appointed to do this. The head was a chap called Ted Sheild, [and we also had] Harold Harding [and] Harold Scott. We got this old house at Riccione which had been knocked about, but it did have a chapel in it, as lots of big Italian houses did. It had plenty of space. I think we had a hundred or so at a time. We had a course which was mapped out by the four of us before we started, and plenty of recreation, because there was a wonderful beach, marvellous for swimming. Other troops went to other places, but we put through a few hundred there.

It was during that time that I had what might be called 'French leave'. Harold Scott and I organised this. As the senior one among us, Ted Sheild signed leave passes for us to more or less go where we wanted, so we set out with the driver. We hadn't been to France, we hadn't been to Paris. It wasn't too far really, because all we had to do was cross the Alps and go through France. We had good jeeps and plenty of petrol. So we went on this jaunt, but we were trapped in a way because we were still in battledress and all the troops in France were in khaki drill. We were conspicuous. We finally got hauled up before the British commission or whatever it was — somebody looking after the troops — and were told to get out within 24 hours, so we did. But we had a lot of fun. We went to one or two shows. I remember going to the opera *Fidelio*. We had a bit of a job once or twice to get through American lines. They'd never heard of us. We lost [Danny Taylor, the driver], but fortunately he turned up again. We were a bit worried at one stage. Of course, he had different, perhaps, interests from what we did in Paris. We don't know what happened but, anyway, he came home.

In 1946 Jack returned to New Zealand.

I came home on the *Mooltan*. The family were there in force at Dunedin railway station. It was great, but it took a bit of settling down. It wasn't long — I had to get back to Tapanui, and that was it. I was absolutely thrilled to be back and to be a civilian again. Some people found it hard, of course, to settle down to home. They'd had a completely free sort of existence and had also experienced life at a different level from anything they would have experienced at home. They took a bit of settling down to the restrictions of normal living, humdrum lack of excitement, the duties of home, and that sort of thing. Some of them got restless, but most of them were glad to be home and face up to life again.

The returned serviceman became a breed, in a way, of its own. They had a common experience that they wanted to share, and the secret of returned servicemen's reunions and things of that kind is to relive and re-share something of that experience, and I think they're entitled to do it. I've always enjoyed doing it with them.

'Padre' was largely a term of affection, although it was the usual word used for a chaplain. 'Chaplain' was more formal. Nobody used it much except in written form for official papers. You were called padre. It was an easy way of addressing a person who was, for the time being, a sort of ex officio officer and at the same time was a sort of father in God, if you like, or father in lots of ways, to the men. So it became a term of affection, and I appreciated that.

It's very hard to comment on how religious the troops were. They were responsive to service. Once we were in action and except perhaps on leave periods, we didn't hang together as a unit. The troops and the squadrons went their own way. They were little units of their own, very often, in action or out of action. I held services wherever it was possible with a group, or a troop, or a squadron, but mainly for troops which were just two or three tanks together with the personnel on them, in just odd places. I think a lot of them came to the services because there was nothing else to do. That's perhaps playing it down a little bit. On the whole, a lot of them attended reasonably well. I didn't force it on them at all. When we were in action and the group was in a particular position and wanted to have some kind of short service, I would go to them and take it. It was very different from when we were in training and had formal church parades.

There are about 700 men in a regiment. It's a lot of people, and they represented a cross-section of New Zealand society.

They certainly had respect for religion if they saw it working out in reality. And the padre was perhaps the flag carrier for that kind of thing. If he carried the flag OK, well, then they respected it.

I didn't get myself involved in welfare work much. It wasn't my thing at all. I did run concerts and shows and try to organise people in leave periods to undertake activities — sport and that sort of thing. I wasn't a purveyor of cigarettes or lollies. My main ministry, as I saw it, was to get to know the people. To be with them, talk to them and, where it was wanted in action, to take the services that were required. In some cases it would be small communion services, in other cases it would be a whole regimental service for those who wanted to come, but the business of the padre being simply a giver out of goodies and things like that, it wasn't my thing.

After his return to New Zealand, Jack continued as minister at Tapanui before being invited to Wellington to serve at St Andrews on the Terrace, where he was minister for sixteen years. He married in 1951, and he and his wife Janet had four sons. In 1964 the family returned to Dunedin, where Jack had been appointed Master of Knox College. He was also Moderator of the General Assembly of the Presbyterian Church of New Zealand and Chancellor of the University of Otago.

'THE BOYS WERE GOOD AND BRAVE PATIENTS'

Isobelle Wright, 807336, Sister, 2 New Zealand General Hospital

Isobelle Wright, the daughter of Rose and James Henderson, was born in Dunedin on 17 October 1914. When Isobelle was six the family moved to Naseby in Central Otago because of her father's ill-health. They later moved to Alexandra so that Isobelle could attend secondary school. After leaving school, Isobelle decided to train as a nurse at Dunedin Hospital. She became a registered nurse in July 1941 and applied to go overseas as a nursing sister soon afterwards, spending some time training at Burnham Camp.

What about from the hospital side of things? Were they willing to let you go?

There were a lot of people more senior than I was. I think in the end it was because I was in a position where I could be replaced. Some of the ones that had been ward sisters for a few years couldn't be released because they were needed. We went to Burnham. There were six sisters and a charge matron there. We weren't busy because we only had the soldiers who were sick, and they weren't very sick — a septic toe, say — it was nothing very serious with them. We never had a full house because they were pretty fit boys waiting to go away. They'd all been vetted before they got in.

Do you recall any significant differences between your time at Dunedin Hospital and army nursing?
No, because we had a sister from Dunedin who had trained us. I think we just carried on the same. Although we were just out of Christchurch, we felt we were in camp and we belonged to that little circle. We felt sorry for people we met in the street who weren't in uniform. We were apart. It was just some feeling that you got. It was the uniform, I suppose.

> *In great secrecy, Isobelle and some other nurses were sent to Wellington Hospital to nurse Japanese prisoners of war who had been wounded during the riot at Featherston Camp on 25 February 1943.*

They didn't clear out one hospital, they took [nurses] from various camps so it wouldn't look so obvious. There was nothing in the papers or radio, no whisper of it. They wanted to keep it quiet. When we got there we found the Red Cross were interviewing the Japanese to see what happened, trying to find out the truth of the whole thing. I think they thought that the Japanese would take retribution on our prisoners.

I can't remember the numbers, but there were quite a few wards full. A lot had been killed. They seemed to separate the officers from the ordinary soldiers. We didn't feel any dislike for them. Of course, we didn't know how our boys had been treated then, either. We felt quite kindly towards them and they got Red Cross rations, cigarettes and chocolate. They were well treated.

You were able to communicate with them?
Yes. They'd talk to the English Red Cross and the New Zealand Red Cross, but not to the Americans. They became quite friendly. One guard we had was a Maori, and in no time at all he could almost speak Japanese — he could understand them and they could understand him. Most of them could speak English if they wanted to. Sometimes they wouldn't. The older ones wouldn't.

They didn't like anything being done for them by a woman, that's one thing I remember. They couldn't bear to be washed by a woman, for instance. No matter how ill they were, they preferred to wash themselves. It was a loss of face, I think. One boy in particular, a young boy, told me that he would be listed as dead. They never listed anyone as prisoners of war. That was a terrible disgrace, which seemed a peculiar attitude to us. One of the things he gave me was a letter — they were so sure they would win the war that this letter was to say that I had looked after the Japanese, and how good I'd been to them. He thought that it would protect me. They had been so indoctrinated, I suppose, that they couldn't visualise [losing], same as we couldn't visualise Britain losing the war.

I can't remember how long we were there, but I don't think it was all that long — it might have been two weeks. Then we went back to Burnham.

Isobelle returned to Burnham and was then posted overseas with the Ninth Reinforcements in 1943.

She left on the Dominion Monarch *with four other nursing sisters and 5000 men.*

I must have known that I was going, because my mother came from Alexandra to Burnham and saw me off. I can see her standing, waving. She was very little. That's the last time I saw her.

The troops were inoculated just ten days before and were having their reaction when they got on board this ship. We went down south and it got very cold. Very cold. A lot of these boys were running temperatures and they got pneumonia. We had quite an influx in the sick bay. It passed within a few days, but they were miserable for a start. The troops were very badly catered for. There was a terrific difference between officers and ORs there. The officers had a lot more comfort and better food, but our officers looked after their boys. They made complaints to the ship's staff. The crew was English.

After arriving in Egypt, Isobelle went to 1 New Zealand General Hospital briefly, and then to 2 New Zealand General Hospital at El Ballah.

We had a lot of boys waiting to go back on hospital ships. We were looking after them. We had one very sad accident there. We used to go to Port Said. There were different concerts and things on there, and there was always an ambulance that would take people down. I didn't go, but there were three VADs, I think, and a sister and some orderlies who had been to a concert and were coming back from Port Said to El Ballah. An American truck came past and took out the whole side of the ambulance and killed all those on that side. The ones on the other side were perfectly all right. It was terrible, so unnecessary. The Americans used to travel very fast.

In October 1943 she got ready to travel with 2 New Zealand General Hospital to Caserta, near Naples.

One of the medical officers married an English girl, and we were helping to give them a bit of a spread after they were married. Some of us went over and made fruit salad and things in the officers' mess.

I went outside and somehow or other I fell into a trench. It was beside where their coppers were and was all black and sooty. It was very dark, I couldn't see a thing. I must have knocked myself out. Of course, I was in a white uniform. Eventually I got up and came inside, and everyone screamed because I'd been crying and had a black face with tear marks dripping down my uniform. Then someone realised my arm was round the wrong way. I had a fracture. There was great consternation then as to what to do. However, in the officers' mess, on the dining table, one of the senior officers gave me an anaesthetic and they set my arm in plaster.

I slept in my tent that night and the wind blew. My hand was pinned up to the tent to keep it elevated, and it went up and down [with the wind]. Next morning it was swollen right up and we were due to go off to Italy. I had to be left behind in a British hospital. I thought I'd be there for the duration of the war, but they sent me up to Cairo and I went to 1GH. The plaster had to be taken off and reset. In due time they sent me to Italy. I'd never been to Italy. There was another New Zealand nurse going over too. We were the only two New Zealanders. It was quite a pleasant trip. I was out of plaster and my arm was all right and I was using it.

We got to Bari and there was a case of smallpox on the ship, so we were put into an English hospital in isolation because they felt we might have made contact with this case of smallpox. However, they did some tests on us and we were released eventually, and then put in an ambulance and taken from Bari to Caserta. It seemed a long drive in the back of an ambulance.

I'll never forget when I got out of the ambulance and looked over and there was Vesuvius erupting. Beautiful. I thought it must always erupt, but it hadn't for years. In the daytime all the cars in Naples had their lights on. You couldn't see anything for the ash afterwards. It was dreadful, but it was quite a sight to see that.

It was a well-established hospital there in a building. There was a British hospital next to it and a POW camp at the side. Then not far away from us was the American hospital. We slept in tents.

We weren't far from Caserta palace, which was military headquarters at that stage. We were probably busier there than we had ever been because we were getting casualties from the war zone, sent down, I suppose, from the Casualty Clearing Stations.

The boys were all in beds in big wards. We might have 40 in a ward. I can remember the screams on night duty. They used to have terrible nightmares. They wouldn't admit to being nervous once you wakened them and quietened them down. They wouldn't say they were scared or overworked. They never complained. They all seemed to be happy with their lot. That was the difference between them and the English army. We did notice that some of them would show photos of their wife and family and were obviously very worried about them. The New Zealanders had no worry about the war at home, although I do remember some of the soldiers talking about how they'd lost their wives. They'd gone off with an American. That wasn't unusual.

Sometimes you would have a rush when a lot were brought down and everyone was terribly busy. Then there'd be a bit of a lull for a while. We used to see the planes going overhead to Cassino from there. They were mainly American.

We must have had a few hundred patients there, thinking of the different wards that they were in. We had some sick boys and boys that died in the hospital, but we did what we could for them. It was the beginning of penicillin, which I think helped a lot of them. In those days it wasn't given by injection or tablet. They would be in plaster and there'd be a tube coming out of their plaster and you syringed the penicillin into the tube and it would go down into the wound. It must have helped a lot of those wounds, stopped septicaemia setting in so they were able to get home. They would probably need more surgery when they got back to New Zealand, but they did quite a lot of surgery at the hospital itself. Amputations.

There was a burns unit. We had a lot of burns. They were always clean. They'd been cleaned up before we got them, and they'd be bandaged too. But the burns were the most horrific injury that I remember coping with, and they were smelly and painful. You'd strip the patients, put them on a sheet and two of us, with an orderly, would lift them into a bath. They would scream with the pain when they got into the saline water. You'd let them soak there for a while and try and lift the bandages off. You picked off as much dead skin as you could and then put this Vaseline-coated perforated gauze on and dressed them. Most of them healed, but it was a pretty painful procedure for the patient. The ones that were burnt in tanks always seemed to have their body burnt, but I can't remember anyone having facial wounds. I suppose they'd be sitting in the tank and that would protect their face, so that would be the last place that would get burnt.

It was the most strenuous nursing I did in that burns unit, because it was steamy and hot. I will always remember that the boys were good and brave patients. Many would not yell out unless something was really radically wrong.

Major General Howard Kippenberger was also nursed at 2 New Zealand General Hospital after being wounded near Cassino.

He had stepped on a mine and badly injured both his legs, which were later amputated. He had special nurses, but I nursed him for a little while when one girl was on leave. He was a very nice patient. Never complained. He was in this special ward and he had — it was his batman really, but he had been a personal friend. When they were there on their own they would call each other by their christian names. He used to have a Don R coming in two or three times a day, running in with messages, and he would write out something and send it back to the division. He was always writing. I don't know if he was writing out notes or telling them how to win the war, or what he was doing. It was the time of Cassino.

He didn't like his nurses changing, so they kept two or three nurses just specially for him. One of them went on holiday, and that's how I came to be in the ward with him. He seemed to accept losing both limbs. They sent him from there to England where he got artificial limbs. In no time at all he was back in that hospital walking through the wards with a stick and talking to these amputees and telling them how easy it was to walk. He was wonderful, really a wonderful man. He did it to show them it was possible. It wasn't the end of the world to have your legs off. I can't remember any other double amputees. I remember lots of single ones. Some of them seemed to be there for quite a long time too, before they got on a boat to get home. We had plenty of morphine, and so if they were in pain they were looked after quite well.

They weren't short-staffed or anything. The theatres were the busiest places when they brought in battle casualties. They could only take so many and they'd always be working long hours to get through.

Because I nursed the burns we had masks. We had gowns and masks on, but the steam wet the masks. They were all infected and I got this dreadful throat. I couldn't swallow. They thought I had scarlet fever, but it was just an infection. I was hospitalised with it. The soles of my feet were raw because the skin all came off them. They sent me to Sorrento to recover. There was a hostel there for all the nurses. It was a beautiful place. I went down there for two weeks, bathed in the Mediterranean, then came [back to the hospital] and had my tonsils out, then went down again for another week. Apart from that I didn't have any health problems. We were all pretty fit. There were never many in the sick bay.

Were you aware of the course of the campaign?

No, not really. All I remember is that the soldiers wanted to get back to the front, which I could never understand. They'd say, 'When can we go back?' and would seem to be upset if they were being sent back to New Zealand. I think they wanted to get back to their mates as much as anything. There was always great rejoicing when a new patient would come in from the same battalion and they'd all be asking about the others. There seemed to be this strong friendship between them, which was quite moving.

We did notice that the English boys were much more reserved and didn't talk to us, whereas the New Zealand boys treated us with respect but had no inhibitions at saying anything to us. The English boys would be reserved even with each other. They didn't seem to have that — well, it wasn't comradeship exactly, but free and easy manner.

I remember on one occasion we had quite a lot of little Gurkhas. They always seemed cold, and they'd huddle down in bed in the red capes that they had. They didn't hold much conversation with us, but they were pleasant and always appreciative of everything. There must have been some action somewhere near that they were involved with. But it was mainly New Zealanders we saw.

Despite the long hours spent nursing, there was also time off.

We must have had entree into the palace because we used to swim in the pool. You would go for walks in the evening out in the country. It was just beautiful.

There must have been quite a lot of poverty down in that part of Italy.

I suppose there was, yes. There were no beggars or anything like that, whereas in Egypt you would see them. They were peasant people and they seemed to live on what they grew. It was poor, but I think if we'd been in Naples we'd have seen more poverty. Out there in the country the children looked well covered and well fed and very cheerful, but some of the Italian children looked very hungry. I always felt awful if you were eating anything in front of them. They'd stand like pitiful dogs. You felt you couldn't swallow it because they looked hungry. Then they'd pick a few wild flowers and come up and give them to you, so you'd finish up giving them your lunch. You had these great big eyes looking at you.

They were very friendly. If we were out walking they'd invite us in and give us a glass of vino or something like that. They were humble people, with a few trees and a few chickens. Not wealthy people at all, but they were quite willing to share what they had with you. They'd always smile at you and talk to you and wave to you, even if you couldn't converse. They'd give you some cherries or some fruit or something. They were generous people, I thought.

We had a donkey derby for the sisters. The Italian [who] worked as a kitchenhand brought his donkey along for me to have a practice for a few days before, and taught me what to do on it. So I won the donkey derby. I've always been passionately fond of donkeys since. The hospital had a football team. They'd arrange a match with perhaps one of the battalions that would come down and play them. All the nursing staff and the VADs would be on the sideline with the orderlies, yelling like mad.

There'd be doctors and orderlies and cooks and all sorts playing in that team. Apart from the football we had a swimming pool which had been made by the unit. That was open to all the hospital. You didn't have to be an officer to use the pool. The Kiwi Concert Party was exceptionally good. Almost everyone went when it was on. The unit put on concerts themselves. They'd have little plays.

We did lots of walking. There were beautiful places to walk in amongst trees, and you'd often take along patients that were up and well, perhaps half a dozen of them. Two or three nurses would go for a walk in the hills and just wander along and discuss life topics. We never talked about war. We talked about the flowers. We always had some flowers in the tent. Every little village had its own cemetery, and all the graves were planted with flowers. That's where we used to collect all our flowers. Everything grew. It was the volcanic soil, I think. Although the frosts were hard in the winter, everything seemed to come away again in the spring. We all had a little garden round our tent.

In the evening you could hear nightingales singing. There were a lot of birds. I remember once seeing a whole lot of swallows, masses of them. They were migrating back to England. Sometimes you'd pick up one on the ground. Some of them didn't make it, and they would just be lying there.

I remember once going to the New Zealand Club and ordering pigeon. I thought I'd get a leg or a wing or something, but it was like a little plucked blackbird on your plate. I had been brought up in Central Otago, where we used to have quail. At least you could get a bone and gnaw something off them, but there seemed to be nothing on these birds. Looking back, I don't remember seeing any sheep or anything like that in the countryside. There was the odd cow, although we never had fresh milk. They always had scraggy-looking dogs, and skinny chickens. If you bought eggs you would never put it in anything to cook straight away, you always put it in a cup because it might have a chicken inside it. They were never very fresh. I think the hens used to run wild and lay anywhere, and then the kids would go out and collect eggs that might have been there for weeks.

We used to have dried potatoes, always mashed. They had no taste whatsoever. I didn't mind the bully beef or the Spam. We were pretty light on vegetables too. Dried eggs was another thing that we used to have. Egg powder made into scrambled egg. I suppose we would eat it when we were hungry — but that scrambled egg and the dried potato. I thought it was wonderful to get a fresh potato, and fresh milk. We used to have dried milk powder, but it wasn't like it is today. It was always very lumpy and you could never get a smooth mix. The dried milk today is quite different.

We got New Zealand Red Cross parcels. There'd be cotton and mending kits in them, which were acceptable. And chewing gum. I don't know why they sent so much chewing gum. And fruit salts, there was always a small bottle of Eno's. There wasn't too much in the line of oysters and whitebait, but the occasional tin would come in. And always a little fruit cake, Ernest Adams, I think. And we did get shortbread and fruit cake sent from our families.

There were occupational therapists amongst the girls. They used to get the boys doing needlework, cross-stitch tapestries. They were sent out from England — a complete package with the wool and everything. Some of the boys would say, 'I'm not going to sew!' but they became very keen and quite good at it. A lot of the doctors even took it up. Then the girls would have leatherwork. If the boys were in plaster and immobile, they would make moccasins and anything to keep their hands going and using things. At one stage they wanted fur to make the moccasins, so somehow or other they got two rabbits. They must have been male and female, because in no time at all we had an awful lot of rabbits in the cages.

One of the other supposed features of Italy was the black market.

Yes. I remember one girl getting into a lot of trouble because she met the matron as she was walking back from the village in her stockinged feet. She had given her shoes, good leather shoes which were bought at the NAAFI, as part payment for some silver that she'd bought. That wasn't considered the right thing to do. We were always supposed to be completely dressed when we went out. Hat and gloves. We weren't really supposed to be out without and this girl was in her stockinged feet, walking home. It was just unfortunate she'd been caught.

One instance I remember in Italy was when we had some British MPs come into the hospital. Apparently there'd been a dance in Naples with an Italian band playing. Then there'd been an alert and a blackout. When the lights went on again the band had no instruments. The drums and everything had gone. They had an idea it was New Zealanders who had taken them, and as we were the nearest New Zealand hospital they thought they might have dumped them with us. But nobody knew anything about it. I think the New Zealanders were noted for their looting. They were pretty good at it. Sometimes I remember Maori boys saying, 'Do you want a car, sister? We'll get a car for you.' Nothing was a trouble.

Can you recall any instances where medical supplies went missing?
No, not really. The drugs had to be accounted for. The senior nurse on duty would have the key to the drug cupboard, and you would have to ask for anything you wanted and sign for it. It wouldn't have been easy. There seemed to be no shortage of drugs. If you wanted a drug for a patient it was always there.

Isobelle remembers going to Rome on leave.

You visited the Spanish Steps and, of course, the Vatican. Mainly churches and art galleries. Pictures that you thought you would never see. They said they'd taken a lot away, but there were a lot of art treasures round Rome. We went through some lovely gardens that belonged to private homes but were open to visits. I remember going to the tearooms where Keats and Shelley used to take tea. We became quite involved with Keats and read up everything we could about him. We went out to the cemetery and saw where they were buried. I suppose I had no great interest in Keats or Shelley before I went to Italy.

We saw the Colosseum and the Forum. I remember all the cats. And the catacombs, of course. We'd go back and back there. I remember it's all dark in there, quite eerie. All these skulls you see set in the wall.

On 2 April 1945 Isobelle and Lawrence Wright were married in a Church of England chapel tent at 2 New Zealand General Hospital. Major Wright was in the New Zealand Medical Corps, and the wedding had been postponed because he had pneumonia. The couple had met in 1939, and after a few dates Isobelle asked him to be her partner at the annual nurses' ball. She saw him intermittently thereafter, as he was in Melbourne until he returned to New Zealand in October 1940. They met again in Egypt in 1941, and kept in touch by letter until Lawrence visited her in El Ballah after the end of the North African campaign.

The man who was going to be best man had gone back to New Zealand, but we had quite a few visitors from regiments that Lawrence had been in down for the wedding. They were entertained and put up at the mess. It was quite a celebration. Sisters offered you bits of civilian clothing that they had, and we went down laden with food to Positano, where we stayed in a house that the British army ran just for honeymoon couples. Anyone who was getting married could book in ahead. It was a lovely place, complete with two Italian maids.

After the war ended, 2 New Zealand General Hospital returned to Cairo.

My husband had been promoted to Senior Medical Officer of the New Zealand troops in Egypt, so we were not far apart. The next six months were relaxed and happy, as we were able to visit Cairo for social functions and dinner-dances.

Sadly, my mother-in-law in Dunedin passed away, and this caused us to revise our plans. We decided to go to the UK for demob so that Lawrence could continue his studies in obstetrics and gynaecology, which he'd given up when he enlisted. So we arrived in London on 30 December 1945, just in time for New Year celebrations.

The couple returned to Dunedin in February 1951, along with their son and daughter, as a result of Lawrence's appointment as Professor of Obstetrics and Gynaecology at the Medical School, a position he held for 30 years.

'LOOK AFTER ONE ANOTHER'

Tautini GLOVER, 802006,
Sergeant, 28 (Maori) Battalion

*Tini Glover, Te Aitanga o Hauiti, the son of
Monarch and Whakaahuru Glover, was born in
Tolaga Bay in December 1923. He was brought up
by his paternal grandparents, and is particularly
grateful to his grandfather for teaching him his
whakapapa and traditional ways, such as fishing
and reading the weather. Tini attempted to enlist
in Gisborne when war was declared, but his
mother found out and stopped him. Keen to get
away, Tini went to Wairoa and enlisted there at
the age of seventeen. After training, he was posted
to Ohaeawai in North Auckland to oppose a feared
Japanese invasion. He went overseas in 1943,
leaving from Wellington on the Nieuw Amsterdam.
Arriving at Port Tewfik, he was sent to camp at
Mena, just out of Cairo, before moving to Maadi
Camp. At the end of 1943 he arrived in Taranto
in southern Italy.*

WE LANDED IN TARANTO AND had to march for miles and
miles with our kit. Halfway between Taranto and Bari

we took over an oak grove at a place called San Basilio. It had an abbey. Monks used to come around asking us for a little food. They used to give us almonds. They had an almond orchard. We made an Advanced Base at San Basilio for the New Zealand troops. They did their training there.

From there we were detailed to join the division at the Sangro. We went up to and crossed the Sangro on trucks, and went to a place called Castelfrentano. It was a factory town. We waited there till our front line troops came out for a rest for Christmas. When they came out we all went into bivouacs. We had to dig a lot of guys out next day because it snowed that night and the tents collapsed. After New Year we moved to the outskirts of Orsogna.

That's when I got wounded — and I'd never even seen a German! We were looking at Company Headquarters. They were getting shelled, and we were laughing because we could see the jokers running out. I was cleaning my rifle. We said just as well they're not shelling us, and the next minute a shell landed about ten or twelve feet away from us. Killed two fellas and wounded three of us. I got my right arm done. My sergeant, who had been in action quite a while, had a butcher's knife and ripped the sleeve off. I remember him putting a field dressing on it. It must have been a big bit of shrapnel because it cut the muscle in half.

I landed at the Advanced Dressing Station. You went to your Regimental Aid Post and from there they took you back to the Advanced Dressing Station. The British paratroopers had a medical team there. They were attached to our battalion for front-line experience because they'd just come out from England. They cleared my arm up and put it in splints. I was there overnight, and next morning I went by ambulance to the Casualty Clearing Station. That's where you first met the nurses and sisters. It was there I had my first wash. This little nurse, Sister Bunny, said, 'I'm going to give you a wash, my boy. How old are you?' I said, 'I'm seventeen, rising 21.' She said, 'You should be still at school.'

I told her that I was going to wash myself — I don't know how I was going to, as I was lying on the bed with my arm in splints. She took all my underwear off and put a rubber sheet over me and a rubber sheet under me. I looked around when she took my boots off and I could see the marks from the socks, being in the snow and sleet and slush. I felt quite ashamed. I hid my face. She was very efficient. I felt very clean. The nursing sisters did a marvellous job. They were true friends.

Tini was sent by Scottish hospital train to 3 New Zealand General Hospital in Bari, where his arm was operated on.

The doctor used what was then the new drug, penicillin. After about three weeks they pulled the plaster off and it was beautiful pink skin. It was all closed up. Within a month I was out of the hospital, then I went to a convalescent depot for two weeks.

From the convalescent depot Tini and his friend, Corporal Cornelius ('Con') O'Brien, were sent back to Advanced Base at San Basilio. Con punched one of the sergeant majors at the base during an argument, and the two men decamped to the nearby Maori Training Depot.

There was an officer, Lieutenant Joe Ngapo of East Coast origin, in charge of the base, and Con told him, 'We've just donged a sergeant major down in base. Can you do anything for us?' He said, 'I can't hide you here. You're lucky there's a reinforcement going to the battalion tonight, so I'll sneak you on that, but you won't be on the list.' He put us on the truck and we got up the line. [The battle for] Cassino was halfway through. They hadn't captured the monastery but they had captured the town, and the Indians were going forward to Castle Hill. We were detailed to go to Mount Cairo. We held the line, but it was a very dangerous position.

We were going up to get into a position to guard this place where the [Germans] were trying to make a cave and put a gun it. It overlooked Route 6, the only way into Cassino, so they reckoned that if they had that gun there they could shoot at Route 6 all the time, put shells down there, and cut Cassino off. Our job was to observe. There were dead bodies outside the house — they were French Ghoums; those are North African, Moroccan, French forces. They were outside and the bodies blew up in the sun. It stunk like hell. We weren't allowed to touch them, because then the Germans would know that we'd been there.

We found two bodies inside the house in a bed. It was the safest place in the house so we dug a hole in the floor and buried the bodies, and then we slept in that room. You didn't think about it, really. You worried about the shelling. There was a platoon of us — about 30. We were there about two weeks and then we were relieved on May Day.

> *Tini recalls some of the German propaganda that was broadcast to the Allied troops at Cassino, in particular one woman, 'Axis Sal'.*

She said, ' Welcome to the New Zealand soldiers. How are you, Kiwis? This is not your war. Why are you poor boys over here? American forces — they've got your girlfriends. Sleeping in your bed at home.' She was well known. She used to speak with a very sexy, lilting voice. 'We've got nothing against you. You've got nothing against Germans. After all, all your top-ranking officers are German — Freyberg, Kippenberger. I know it's supposed to be a secret move of yours, but we know you're here. I'll play a song for you — "Now is the Hour". They're saying goodbye to the American soldiers going to the Islands, but another lot will be in to take your bed.' It was demoralising sort of talk.

And what did you used to think when you heard that?
Silly bitch.

> *After he came out of the line at Cassino, the authorities caught up with Tini and discovered that he was absent without leave from Advanced Base, so he and his friend Con were sent back there. Their 'punishment' was to return to the battalion.*

We missed the campaign to Sora up the Liri Valley. We saw part of it, but we were pulled out from there and sent to a place called Arce, a rest area, all ready to go into the Florence campaign.

At Arce they had swimming sports in a big dam. We cleaned up the whole lot because we had those Rotorua fellas and they were all good swimmers. At Arce they taped off a patch of potatoes and maize. We weren't allowed to touch it because it belonged to the Ities. The Ities used to look at their maize and their potatoes every day and, no, good soldiers. But soldiers used to go in at night. The [first] four rows, the cobs looked nice but the day before we left there, the Ities went down to have a look — not a lot of blinking cobs in the centre. And they looked at their potatoes — just the stalks. There were no spuds underneath them. We were having a cook-up every night.

In Italy, we found puha. We used to get it in a kerosene tin and cook it with spuds, get a tin of bully beef to flavour it, or a tin of bacon. The Americans had fat bacon, so a tin of fat bacon in there used to be rather good.

Did you have much to do with the Italians when you were at Arce?
They used to come through the lines for washing. We were invited to their homes for a drink, but no sex or anything like that. They got on well with the New Zealanders, and the New Zealanders were pretty kind-hearted in their own way. I saw one of our jokers get a hell of a hiding one night from his own mates. He'd tried to muck around with a woman who was up the family way and she'd just lost her husband. He tried to hop into bed with her and he got thrashed. So there was an honour amongst soldiers.

We hopped on the truck. We didn't know where it was going to take [us] but, as it happened, we were confronted with a little castle town called Tavarnelle. It was Sunday, and rather than go there in the dark they sent forward a reconnaissance patrol to probe the enemy, to see where they were. They went right up to this castle and heard tanks inside, so they came back and told us. It was getting dark by the time they come back so we attacked straight away, along a company front. And we captured the town of Tavarnelle. We didn't capture the tank; that ran away.

Tavarnelle had a shop I remember well. They had those steel shutters that lift up on the stores, but what we used to do was get a landmine with a hand grenade. The landmine had TNT in it, high explosive, with a hand grenade attached to it. We'd go somewhere far away and, with a line, pull the pin out of the hand grenade, and that would explode and blow the shopfront out. That's how we got into shops. This shop happened to be a music shop and everybody got a piano accordion. All the jokers, beside having their rifles, had a piano accordion each, until they got too heavy, then they threw them away. There were a lot of piano accordions in the division, and that's how they got them. They never paid for them.

We went beyond there. Nepia Mahuika was our officer. We went into a grove of trees for the night, and in the morning he told us to go across this slope. We were halfway across and he said, 'Get back! Get back into the copse of trees.' As soon as we got back, down came the screaming meemees, six-barrel mortars, and peppered the whole area. We would have all died except for Nepia. I said to him, 'Nep, why did you send us back?' He said, 'Well, I thought about getting the cows in, in Ruatoria. When I go to get the cows, early in the morning, the birds are singing, and they've got their wings down, drying themselves on the top of the trees in the sun. I didn't hear a bird.' Now, that's from the old people. That's an inheritance, in my opinion. Bushcraft is there. He was a good man.

They continued up the slope.

There was a chap from Otago yelling out for us to help him. He was bringing a chap out. He had no legs. He'd stood on a landmine. He begged Boy Tomoana to shoot him. I don't know what happened, but he died. We took over D Company's house.

Next morning we shifted from there. We got a call that Tiger tanks were seen on the ridge and one of our platoons was in difficulty. They were pinned down and we had to go up and get them. I saw a lot of dead bodies on the way up. Our boys. Counted about six of them.

We went up a long, winding hill, and when we got up there our 13 Platoon was there. There were many casualties. The Germans let us through. Three or four of us. Then our platoon sergeant was bringing up our main force, and that's when the [Germans] attacked him with a machine gun. Smashed his arms. It was a bloody mess. He was lying on the ground, moaning and groaning, and his brother said to me, 'I'm going down to look at Charlie.' I said, 'He's all right. He's a bit over the ridge. He's lying down.' But he went down to pick him up. I thought, if it was my brother, I'd go. He went to pick Charlie up and the next minute, the machine gun opened up. I said to Whiro Tibble, 'I've got it in my sights, Red.' He said, 'What the hell are you waiting for?' And I peppered the [haystack] and got that joker. He threw his arms up, and then two jokers crawled out and went running up the hill. One was running as if he had a crook leg, and I shot them both. I'd wondered what it was like to shoot a man. You didn't get pleasure out of it, but satisfaction that you'd done a job.

One tank was oozing around the top, and we were frightened he might put an incendiary into the haystack we were hiding under. That's what they did at times — put an incendiary shell in and you'd get burnt. As we were crossing a field towards the road, a chap came from behind a heap of wood and went to shoot Whiro Tibble. I had my machine gun slung on my shoulder, in position, all ready, and I fired it, and I got him. That made four. And Red Tibble thanked me. We got into this stable and that's when we got smacked with hand grenades and I got it in the head. Even a little head wound bleeds like anything.

We escaped. I broke my trouser crutch, I was going that fast. Anyway, we got down and Red got wounded. It was a beautiful wound — through the lips, through the nose, through the eyebrow. One bullet. We all ended up in Siena in the hospital. It wasn't a building, it was a long tent.

Tini was sent to Senigallia on the Adriatic coast to recuperate, but managed to convince the doctor to send him back to the battalion.

When I got back they were in Florence. I enjoyed myself in Florence. They had a Forces Club in Florence and I met some nice women there. They were not brothel women, they were women that wanted — food was what they wanted. It was a bad, bad situation.

Then we shifted over to the Adriatic coast to a place called Cattolica. Our job was to capture the Rimini airfield, which we did. We went beyond that and cut the Rimini–San Marino railway line. The Canadians had a go before us and, man, they were piled up in this defile. Dead. They got slaughtered. They did the heavy part and we went through them in the morning.

Then we went into the attack on Faenza. When we got to Forli we had a big church service and went in that night on Faenza. We lost a lot of boys. It was a bad time.

The Germans were consolidating in Faenza, giving us a hard time. We couldn't capture it front on. We kept to the flat on the east of Faenza. As we were moving up to the start line, our artillery were firing through the trees and we lost a couple of guys. Our orders were to get to the start line at twelve o'clock. We were there at the start, following a creeping barrage.

On the open flank there was a railway line, and 15 Platoon was detailed to break up into three lots. I had the section which was mopping up the rear, and we also had to look after the open flank along the railway line. We did very well. We went along. I had a lot of new boys with me that night. One of them was a machine-gunner, Dooley Swann. During the attack I could hear the Bren gun — we used to call it the 'sardine tin' because it doesn't make a lovely noise like the Spandau. I went over and said, 'What are you fellas firing at?' 'We're just seeing that our machine guns work.'

We captured a lot of Germans there. It was a mess. The

Germans were running everywhere, making a nuisance of themselves. They didn't want to fight. They wanted to give in. They wanted us to pay attention to them, but we had too much on our minds. We were trying to get our tanks up, but they wouldn't move. We were lucky, we had a lot of partisans there. They wanted to get rid of the Germans too. That's when the orders were given: take no prisoners if there are too many to handle. I couldn't do that. I can't kill a man in cold blood.

The next morning I was evacuated. I wasn't wounded or anything. Faenza was taken.

I had my 21st birthday in Faenza. It was Christmas 1944. The muttonbirds arrived in patriotic parcels; and beautiful fruit cakes. I remember them well. I had a balaclava and a pair of knitted socks. A tin of Andrews liver salts. Now, you mightn't think that was much of a thing, Andrews liver salts. We made fritters and scones, and that was our baking powder. You could get flour from the Italians, but there was no raising ingredients, and your Andrews liver salts did that. Oyster fritters. If there was a tin of salmon, we stuck that in and had a seafood fritter. The South Island platoons used to get their own muttonbirds and oysters.

We took over Faenza and were in a big three-storey place. I had a cousin, Joey Maurere, who was a storeman in the cookhouse. He said, 'We've got some muttonbirds. I'll pinch some.' We went up to the top storey and were cooking the muttonbirds in a kerosene tin. Every five minutes I went down in the street and sniffed the air, hoping that they wouldn't smell our muttonbirds. But little did we realise that the quartermaster sergeant had known that Joey pinched these muttonbirds.

Once the birds were cooked the quartermaster sergeant came and took them off Tini and his friends — although he did leave them one each.

We had our feed of muttonbirds. On Christmas Eve they had a big party and the Germans sent some shells in and hit Battalion Headquarters in Faenza. Two or three of the guys got killed. Phil Campbell, from the Kiwi Concert Party, who was visiting, was one. It was a one-off thing — they managed to range their long guns.

We were holding the line there for a while. The Senio stopbanks were just further on, and we made a line on the first lot of stopbanks. The Germans made a sort of stand there. They used to come up to the stopbanks and have a go at Faenza in the distance, early in the morning.

At that time I was in the offing of taking over my new job as clothing corporal, but I was still in the front line.

Was it quite safe in Faenza?
They shelled in the morning, shelling some of the buildings, but they weren't getting us really. They had no aircraft. And from then on, it was all go — onto the Lombardy Plains and away. That was my last show, Faenza. Thank goodness. I saw my share. A lot of people were over there for years and saw nothing, but in eighteen months or two years, I saw a lot. Got wounded three times.

We served our time. A lot of our officers used to say, 'You volunteered to fight the war. These Pakehas, a lot of them are conscripts, so they've got no obligation to fight the war, but you have to.' This is our price of citizenship. That's when that term, 'price of citizenship', came out, coined by A.T. Ngata. In other words, to us, we were second-class citizens until such time as we fought for our friends and proved to them that we could fight.

What other things did your officers used to tell you before you went into action?

'Well, boys, the honour and the glory of all your family.' They used to talk about our forefathers being fighters. 'Never turn your back on the enemy.' That was drilled into us all the way. 'Look after one another.' 'Blood is thicker than water.' That's why I think we were so good, because we fought in blood lots. You'd go and help. I always had a mate there who was a relation of mine. We all went to school together. Being related made it hard when soldiers were wounded or killed, however. You had your cry and you buried them with love and tenderness. You put your hand on their face. When they're sleeping, they're sleeping. I never thought I could handle dead men, but I can handle any dead, even now.

The Maoris didn't like the name of Hori, but the South Island, 23 Battalion, they'd say, 'Here are my Hori cobbers.' We didn't mind them, they were allowed to. 'What outfit are you in, boy?' '23.' 'Well, that's all right.' They got on the drink like us. They got on well with us.

Tini remembers a lot of looting in Italy.

I would never loot a soldier. The only time I did was when I said to a German officer, 'You've got a good watch there.' He said, 'I was expecting you to take it.' I said, 'I'm asking you to give it to me because once you go back, those jokers behind will take it off you. Better to give it to me. I'm the front-line soldier.' I got a camera off a German officer. He said, 'Please, here's my camera, but leave my photos. Let me have my wedding photos and my photos of my children.' I let him take his photos and I brought that camera home. It was a Zeiss, a good camera. I always asked them; I've never taken things.

I've seen officers shot and lying with their Luger [pistol]. I always called a mate of mine, 'Hey, there's some dollars here, lying on the ground.' [My friend] used to go out looting, and he'd say, 'I'll give you a few bob when I sell it.' I didn't take things off a dead man. The Americans paid big money. They used to come around asking if we had any guns for sale, had we got any war souvenirs.

The Maori Battalion was well known for pinching German weapons.

You had to hand those weapons in after every action, but we used to hide ours in the food trucks. Out of a section of twelve men, you were only supposed to have two automatics. Your section leader had a Tommy gun, and you had a Bren gun, but when the Maoris went into action, out of the twelve, I think there was only about two rifles. All the other eight either had German guns or extra Bren guns, also extra Tommy guns. The Tommy gun was inaccurate and didn't go very far. Bren guns were very accurate. You could snipe with Bren guns. I loved my Bren. Mine was official because I was section leader.

I've never been in a bayonet charge, but I've pulled my bayonet to give a joker a jab in the backside when he wouldn't do as he was told. Some of them get stubborn, Hitler Youth jokers. Young fellas, seventeen, eighteen. They were arrogant and said, 'You can't hurt us. We're the master race.' That's when we'd pull our bayonets out and give them a jab in the bloody backside. 'We'll show you whether you're the master race. Can you feel that?' They didn't say too much after that.

Tini does not remember very many men being unable to go into action.

A joker came running down the stairs and said he couldn't take it, so we left him in a corner and said, 'Stay there.' But we were all frightened. I tell you what, I never heard a haka. Somebody asked me, 'Did you haka when you went into action?' I said, 'Not haka really.' But we screamed. We screamed like devils and I think that was our inheritance coming out. The old people. As soon as we went in and saw a German, we started yelling. It's a queer scream, a high scream. We screamed at the top of our voices. And some Germans got paralysed behind their guns. I've seen them, many a time, attacking and the joker behind the gun, with that scream, it put him off. He'd got his hands up. 'Ka mate, ka mate', we had no time for that; but that scream, it seemed to help us.

There was plenty for the men to do when they were out of action.

We had our own truck. Te Rau Aroha was donated by the Native School children of New Zealand with their pennies. They used to pull up anywhere. We'd get a shock when we saw them, places where we wouldn't expect them. Pull up and might have a few smokes and lollies, nothing out of the ordinary. And cups of tea when we were in a static area.

And we had the New Zealand film unit, Mobile Cinema Unit. They gave us good pictures. We used to see the New Zealand news — those Home Guards marching up a lane. All the boys would say, 'Boo. Bloody Home Guard.' And we saw the [Te Moananui-a-Kiwa] Ngarimu investiture at Ruatoria. I saw my mother on film. We saw people returning to New Zealand. That was really good. The Yanks used to lend us the latest films, then when the Kiwi Concert Party came in, they'd go over to the Yank quarters and give a couple of shows for them. We'd sort of swap with them.

Did lots of men go to the brothels?
Yes. When we got to Camerino there was a little town where they had the postal service, Fabriano. That was a brothel town. We used to go along to the Red Cap headquarters [and] ask them, 'Hey, where's the best brothel in town?' 'You go to this brothel. They're quite clean girls there.' We took a young joker and said, 'C'mon. We'll initiate you.' He said, 'No, I don't want to go. I've never had a girl before.' We took him to a house that we knew and told the woman to give him the works because she was a woman who knew her way, she knew all the tricks of sex. We paid for him and he went in. He didn't want to. He was there for about ten minutes and he came out with his hair hanging down — because we all had long hair — and his battledress coat off. He was hanging onto his trousers, his braces were down, and he said, 'Can any of you jokers lend me another ten shillings?' He was wanting an encore. We said, 'Little

bit at a time, young fella. Don't overdo yourself. That's enough for this time.' He said, 'Oh please. Give me ten shillings.' She dragged him into the room and they were there for another ten minutes or so, and he came out again and said, 'God, that was good.' We said, 'How did you pay for it?' He said, 'She took my underpants and singlet.'

After coming out of action at Faenza, Tini was transferred to the Quartermaster's Store and became the battalion's clothing sergeant. The job involved making sure that the troops were not selling bits of their uniform and that they were all issued with their full uniform, especially when there was a muster parade. In due course he arrived in Trieste and spent some months there before moving to Lake Trasimene. Like many of the troops, Tini had met a woman in Trieste.

We tidied up in Trieste, I said goodbye to Lydia, my girlfriend, which was sad, and we went down to Lake Trasimene. A lot of those Trieste women followed us to Trasimene. We were there for a while, then we went into winter quarters in Florence — that's where we handed all our weapons in. That was a big job for us, because we had to check off all the compasses and guns and everything. We were about a month there.

Tini, along with the rest of the Maori Battalion, went back to base camp near Bari on 6 December 1945, then left for Egypt on the Dominion Monarch *on Boxing Day. After picking up some troops at*

Port Tewfik, they sailed for home. Tini returned to Tolaga Bay and worked in the area for some time, before taking up an opportunity to train as a carpenter through the Rehabilitation Department. He worked in the Hutt Valley, and eventually had his own building business before returning to Gisborne, where he worked in the freezing works for many years. He studied at Massey University and the Hawke's Bay Community College at Taradale, and retired from the freezing works as cleaning foreman.

Tini remembers his arrival back in New Zealand very clearly. The ship arrived off Wellington on 23 January 1946 but could not get into port because of heavy seas and fog.

We had a hell of a job getting into Wellington. We were supposed to march through the city, 28 Battalion, but instead of getting in at seven o'clock in the morning, we never got in till two o'clock in the afternoon. The ship berthed at Pipitea Quay. We marched from there to Aotea Quay, and the Ngati Poneke Club had a big reception for us there. Several of our ex-colonels were there to welcome us.

We dispersed that night after a nice meal. I remember coming back on the train. It was a long trip, and we hit Matawhero early in the morning, and they said, 'Don't allow them in until eight o'clock, because we're not ready for them.' We were supposed to go to the railway station and march almost two miles through the town to Poho-o-Rawiri Marae. And the boys starting smashing the railway carriages because we were so near home yet we'd been told to stay there till they were ready. So they brought us in.

My mother and father were there, and my young sister who I hadn't seen. I was not allowed to break ranks. We marched in and I saw my mother and father there, and this little girl. I heard this girl say, 'Which one's my brother, Dad?' He must have pointed to me. We were still standing to attention, listening to speeches, and she came and held my hand and said, 'Are you my brother?' 'Yeah.' She said, 'You've been a long time coming home.'

'I'm home now.'

'THE MOST TERRIBLE
GAME OF ALL'

GORDON SLATTER, 441668,
PRIVATE, 26 BATTALION

*Gordon Slatter was born in Christchurch in
1922. When he was a boy, Gordon and his family
moved to Masterton, where he spent the rest of
his childhood. He had fond memories of growing
up in a small town. After leaving school, he
began studying for an arts degree at Canterbury
University College. At the age of eighteen, Gordon
was called up. He went into camp as a member
of 1 Canterbury Regiment at Addington Raceway
after completing his university exams in November
1941. He then trained at Burnham Camp until
1944, when he went to Italy and joined A Company
of 26 Battalion.*

I WENT AWAY TO THE war wondering what it would be like —
how would I react? I was frightened most of the time but
sometimes, for some unknown reason, I got quite brave, and
I still don't know why. I came away from it still wondering —
why did I do that? Is it adrenaline? Is it madness? I give
the reason that you're frightened of running away and your

cobbers would know, but there must be more to it. Sometimes I was scared stiff and absolutely panicked, other times I could be quite brave. I thought, If I'm lucky I mightn't get it. But death can strike in some strange ways. One bloke went out to chop some firewood in the middle of winter and caught his axe on a tripwire. I don't know how they told his mother about that — he'd be Killed in Action, I suppose. Another time I found myself in the biggest paddock in all Italy. Usually it was close fighting — grapevines and houses and villages — and you couldn't see much. You could hear what was going on but you couldn't see what the front platoons were doing, or the platoons on each flank, but here we emerged in this huge paddock, and the whole of 6 Brigade was crossing it. For the first and only time in my life I saw a brigade advancing. It was like a military drill. And then, of course, the Germans opened up and I thought, Oh, they won't pick on me. Why should they? They've got all these other jokers. I didn't feel scared at all until they started up with the mortars. A mortar is a remorseless bloody thing and it comes straight down on top of you. They're the most frightening things. I ran for the nearest house. We had a new sergeant major and he said, 'Come back!' I said, 'Bugger you.' I looked back and he was following me. There's something tempting about a big stone casa with thick walls. I was trying to dig in with my trenching tool and I thought, No, I'm not staying here, not under mortars.

We were in the house because we were Company Head-quarters, but the platoons were dug in, in case of a counterattack. One chap who had been wounded a few weeks before came back, dug his hole, got into it, got out in the middle of the black night and got hit in the bum by a bullet. Now, you make any sense out of that. I came away from the war as puzzled about it as when I went in.

Gordon was happy to remain a private.

I didn't want the responsibility of making decisions that might take other men into danger. I was quite happy to follow the man in front and not be too heroic and do what I was told to do. And hope that I would survive.

It was all a matter of luck, I suppose. I had a very good friend who I went away with, and we got into a house on the morning of 20 December 1944. It was right by a crossroads. We had a bulldozer working on it, and of course the Germans heard the bulldozer and they zeroed in on this. I was sleeping upstairs — I never did it again — and I suddenly had a premonition. I woke up and I thought, Something bloody awful's about to happen. So I got halfway down the stairs and mortars came in through the open roof. I dived under the table. Shorty Smith was lying next to me and he said, 'Hell, I'm hit!' And he was. I learnt later on that my close friend Ron Clark had gone outside and into the haystack, and a mortar shell landed in the yard and he was killed in his sleep. Well, I hope he was.

Our morale was a bit low at that stage. It only takes a few casualties, your own personal friends — it takes a bit of getting over, that does.

But we were rotated. You had a fortnight in the line, and then a week back in Faenza or Forli. You had a hot shower and change of underwear and you were a different man. You'd go off to the NAAFI for a beer and listen to an Italian band.

The Kiwi Concert Party were up there, and they were always a civilian show. They never put on any uniforms like the British ENSA did, it was always a civilian show to take your mind off the war. It was, I suppose, a time when the bad times were terrible and the good times were fantastic.

In April 1945, along with the rest of the New Zealand Division, 26 Battalion was fighting in the area to the east of Bologna. The Germans had established a number of 'Lines' in the area, one of which was the Genghis Khan Line on the Idice River.

I sometimes think that I was the man who broke the Genghis Khan Line. A Company came up on the left of the other companies, approaching this river — it was meant to be the Genghis Khan Line. I was 'I' bloke and I carried the map board. We were so far left that I'd led us into the Polish territory. There was a ford and we found we could paddle across it, so I reckon I broke the German Genghis Khan Line. They told Freyberg that that's where we were and there was a great argument back at Div Headquarters. Freyberg said, 'We can't stay there, we'll get shot up by the Poles when they come up.' Brigadier Parkinson, with a sly grin, is supposed to have said, 'Well, we broke the Hindenburg Line by sneaking a man through,' and the general grinned and gave way and said, 'Right, well, they can stay there and then we'll get our tanks across.' So I had the great pleasure of seeing our tanks go across that ford. It was A Squadron of 20 Armoured. We were the first troops across and that turned the line. Bologna was only a few miles further on to the left.

Gordon is interested in what it is that makes a good soldier or a brave soldier, and whether there was anything special about the New Zealand Division.

New Zealand soldiers had a sardonic sense of humour. You know, belittling themselves and being cynical about objectives. We made mock of the leaders and their pompous phrases. We respected our officers, those that had proved themselves in particular, but we didn't kowtow to them or think we were inferior in any way. When I was there, sergeants and corporals didn't sew on stripes. They led. You knew who they were, and you followed them. Of course, a cynic would say that was because they didn't want to get sniped, and that might be so, but the fact was that they didn't boast about rank or think it was important, and they didn't skite about what they'd done.

The most unlikely people can become heroes. I met two men who'd both won both the MC and the MM — as an officer and as a sergeant. Both of them were short, skinny and wore spectacles, so they didn't look military or brave and they never spoke about how they'd got those medals. They must have just been natural soldiers. It's a world of its own, and you can't prophesy who's going to do what until they get there.

People ask me why our division was so good. There were plenty of other good ones too, but I think we had something extra, and it was explained to me by a soldier who happened to be my officer in the 1 Canterbury [Regiment]. He was in the first battle in Italy, around Orsogna, and he had a feeling that things weren't right. They were billeted in a house and he went out to where the German lines were and came back to see if he would get challenged. He got right up to this soldier, who didn't challenge him. And he told him off a treat, 'Why didn't you challenge me?' The soldier was crying. It was his first action. He said, 'Sir, I couldn't see you.' 'What do you mean, you couldn't see me?' 'I'm night blind.' He said, 'Well, you shouldn't be out here.' And the soldier said, 'But it was my turn and the other fellas are tired.' The next morning they advanced and they got caught in a mortar stonk, and this officer was wounded and the soldier was badly wounded. He was dying. So the officer crawled over to him to see what he could do, and that young soldier said to him, 'Would you take my boots off, sir?' He said, 'Why on earth do you want your boots off?' 'So I won't be too heavy for the fellas carrying me out.'

Well, I reckon that story illustrates why the New Zealand Division was so good. An officer was concerned for his men, and the men were concerned for their mates. It was so formidable because of that feeling between the ranks and the concern for each other. Anybody who served in that division had the mark on them for the rest of their lives. It was a slice of New Zealand transplanted overseas, and the same men worked their way up through the battalion.

Gordon remembers entering Trieste at the end of the war.

We were out in front, and we were wondering if we would have to chase the Germans or whether they would surrender. There was a long convoy and we were part of it. Not at the sharp end, because Divisional Headquarters was back a bit. We became very aware, once we'd crossed the Isonzo, that it was a different atmosphere. We started to see the red flag and these different-looking soldiers who we found out later resented the fact that we'd moved across what they'd hoped would be their border, into what they thought would be their territory.

The old joke was that the Germans wanted to surrender to the New Zealanders because they'd only lose their watches. If they surrendered to the Yugoslavs, they'd lose their lives. I didn't see a great deal of that. I think 22 Battalion and the armoured regiments went right into the city and took over what Germans were eager enough to surrender. I saw more of them as we approached Trieste, when they were put behind wire. I've always remembered a squad of Gurkhas with a Vickers gun guarding them, and you could almost see those Gurkhas willing those jokers to make a break for it. Of course, they had more sense than that. I saw more of the Germans before the final surrender, but then again I'd never even seen a German until I went to Italy. During the Italian campaign the fighting was mostly at night, a few shadowy figures, that sort of thing. Sometimes you'd spot them over the river doing something or other. I didn't have a great deal to do with them, but we had a healthy respect for them, I'll say that. They were great soldiers, great soldiers. They must have been to fight all that way up that peninsula, river by river. They were tough.

I saw German prisoners, and I used to look at them and think, What a motley-looking lot compared to — here's nationalism, if you like — compared to our neat uniform, our battledress. They seemed very scruffy, but then the paratroopers in particular wore an overall sort of thing. They didn't look particularly smart, but they were great soldiers. We had one in our Company Headquarters at one stage, and because I was the intelligence bloke at the time, I was supposed to ask him a few things, so I asked him how it was that an officer and a paratrooper could surrender like that. And he stood to attention and said, 'I know war, I was in Cassino, but these flame-throwers, they are not war.' Tough luck. They used flame-throwers with great eagerness wherever they went.

When they entered Trieste, A Company was attached to Divisional Headquarters as a guard because of the difficult situation.

We were detached from the battalion and went in with the Divisional Headquarters convoy into the castle at Miramare. The city itself seemed to me something like Wellington and something like Auckland. It was a most attractive-looking city. From the castle battlements we could look out over the Gulf of Venice, and see all the fishing boats with their coloured sails. It made a big impact on me.

Lieutenant General Bernard Freyberg used Miramare castle as Divisional Headquarters.

We used to see him every day, and go for a swim with the general, which seemed a very democratic thing to do. I couldn't imagine it happening in the British Army. [I remember] looking down at these demonstrating mobs of people, either waving the red, white and green banners of Italy or the red star of Yugoslavia. There were people getting hit on the head, shots being fired, people running for their lives, that sort of thing.

That was a bit disturbing to look at. We were there until we were relieved by C Company and we moved back into the hills, which wasn't quite so pleasant as the situation was getting very precarious at that time.

Gordon recalls his impressions of the Yugoslav partisans.

I thought of them as sort of guerrillas. They were wearing a mixture of American and British and Russian equipment. There were women striding along in the ranks, and initially we'd got a great admiration for them for the way they'd come right across the mountains and the war they'd fought, but they seemed to become rather truculent and aggressive, I suppose, and it was a sort of cat and mouse situation — wherever we shifted a platoon into a house, they would shift one in opposite. If we put a tank there, they'd bring in one of their little ones to oppose it, and so on. We had to carry arms everywhere, even to a race meeting, and I think we felt that we'd just finished one war, and didn't want to be starting another one, and we rather resented the whole thing.

The average New Zealander had no knowledge of the Yugoslav language but he had a working knowledge of Italian, and it's far easier to get along with an Italian signorina in a two-piece bathing suit than a Yugoslav lady with hand grenades in the belt, so straight away there was an instant sympathy with the Italians, whom we knew right the way through the peninsula. New Zealanders are a pragmatic lot; they said, 'Well, 90 per cent of the population [of Trieste] is Italian, so it should be an Italian city.'

Our Vickers platoon had to mount their machine guns overlooking the racecourse while we had a race meeting. I thought, Well, that wouldn't happen at Addington. What also sticks in my mind is eating lovely, big, ripe, red cherries up in the hills behind Trieste.

The other thing I can remember is guarding a building in Trieste. I got a deckchair and put my Tommy gun against the wall and was reading a book, and along came a British officer. There was an English soldier with blancoed web gear, and he saluted, presented arms and all this, but [the officer] said something to me. I said, 'Oh, it's just in there.' I thought, I'm not going to jump up for him. We're not in his bloody army. Which was totally incorrect, but anyway that's how we felt. It was that colonial independence we had.

After we'd crossed the Reno we sat on the bank to dry our socks. It was a beautiful day so we all stripped off to our underpants, and we were sitting there, listening to the dance music on the BBC, illegally on the radio. Along came a scout car and out got an officer of the 6 British Armoured Division. He was immaculate. He came over — I was the nearest one to him — and he said, 'Where is your commanding officer?' I said, 'That's George, over there.' So he went to this group of Kiwis and he was throwing tentative salutes, very embarrassed — and he got away as quick as he could from George, because he couldn't understand that an officer should sit in his underpants with his men and just be one of them. That was George Murray, a great soldier.

Gordon remembers how the troops spent their leave in Trieste.

I've read official books saying that the venereal disease rate was the highest that the division had ever known, which was probably true, but I honestly don't know anybody in our unit that had it. Now, I could be naive, there could have been others in other companies or other platoons that had it — we used to joke that you weren't a man till you'd had it three times — but I honestly didn't know anybody. If there was an increase in sexual activity, and no doubt there was — this was at the end of a long and arduous campaign and suddenly there we were in one of the cosmopolitan cities of the world with these absolutely glamorous young Italian ladies, sunbathing on the beach and so on. It would be inevitable, and I daresay there would be people who did get VD all right, but as I say, I didn't know anyone personally. I knew plenty of people who went off to the brothels, but they were well catered for before they left. You were supposed to pick up prophylactics from the RAP before you went. I didn't come across the licentious soldiery that people talked about so much, but if men did indulge, well, good on them. They'd earnt it, I suppose you could say. Certainly, I think some Italian women were taken advantage of because they were poor, their husbands perhaps killed or in prisoner of war camp. And a lot could be got for a bar of soap or a stick of chocolate or an army blanket. They weren't angels, they were 40,000 virile men flung into this environment.

For a young fella of 22, it was the highlight of my life, I suppose. The war was over, we had at the back of our minds that we were going to go to Japan, but that could wait, and once that fear of the Yugoslavs and the Germans had gone, it was a great existence. All we lived for was swimming, having a few beers and going to the pictures. We ended up in one of the great cities of Europe. Not in the first class like Venice or Florence, but still a lovely place. Beautiful beaches, lovely climate, friendly population, an opera house and picture theatres. It was like a leave centre.

We went from there and got dumped into some dusty paddocks at Trasimene, and that was a terrible blow. We knew we were destined to go to the Pacific, and I know people jump up and down about the atom bomb. That was a dreadful thing to do to any city, I know — we all know that — but I might not be sitting here if it hadn't happened. I think a lot of us knew if we had to take part in an invasion of Japan, it would be a terrible business for us. That was a very real fear. And yet, when we got the news of the atom bomb and the Japanese surrender, there wasn't any wild celebration in our lot. We just sort of sat there and thought, Well, wonder what's going to happen next? What sort of world are we moving into? But it was a sense of great relief that we wouldn't be shipped off to the Pacific.

We had a great respect for the Italian country people, who seemed a different breed from the townspeople, I thought. That may be true in most countries. The country people were marvellous, simple folk, who worked all day, dawn to dusk. Women behind the plough. We were inclined to think that the women were the backbone of Italy. We didn't have a great deal of time for Italian men, who seemed to stride along the road carrying nothing while the women toiled along. I found the city people more flashy and quicker to make a buck out of you, whereas the country people would be genuinely hospitable. Of course, we did things for them. We brought them soap and chocolate, and they did our washing and that sort of thing.

They gave us meals. They were very good people, I thought. They were very strict with their daughters, too.

I think the average Kiwi treated the Italian womenfolk pretty well and was sorry for them. I saw a pregnant woman carried to the rear in a wheelbarrow, and [there was] one famous instance where two soldiers tended to a lady in labour, in a ditch, during an advance. It was said they were farmers and knew what to do. The civilians I saw were being evacuated from the houses that we occupied in the front. We only saw them in Forli and Faenza largely. In the rest areas we cultivated them because it was a great thing to go to a farmhouse and get eggs. A soldier's life seemed to consist mainly of trying to find eggs, and Mama would cook up a great big omelette and if we had a tin of Bluff oysters, all the better — in that would go too. We would go to these farmhouses to get washing done, to get a meal away from army cooking. We treated those people with respect, and they expected that, too. They had a certain dignity. They were simple people who lived close to the land.

Of course there would be some — and we always tended to think it would be the blokes in the rear areas — who would take advantage of their poverty and bribe them into sex, and so on. I didn't see a great deal of that in our outfit. We were more interested in getting fed than anything, and if we could turn up with a bar of chocolate to be converted into food, that was good. You'd go to this farmhouse and feel that you were in a home situation. Of course, they'd all be yawning by nine o'clock because they'd be up at dawn behind the plough. I'll always remember, too, going to a house in Trieste. An English seaman took me along there because he'd got friendly with them, and these two little girls sang 'The Blue Danube' in

Italian. Lovely. The Italians have marvellous children. Beautiful children. They said, 'The next time you come, you've got to sing a New Zealand song,' so I thought I'd front with 'Pokare Kare Ana' or 'Mehe Manu Rere'. When we were at school we sang Maori songs. But I never got to go again.

Being inclined towards history, Italy made a big impression. The old bridges, the old cathedrals and places that I saw. During the war, I didn't actually get to the showplaces. I was billeted in Florence so I knew Florence, but I didn't get Rome leave and I didn't see Naples. I certainly got to Venice, because we went past Venice on the day it was liberated, and I'll never forget my first sight of Venice. It was like a city floating out to sea.

I wasn't a great believer in the war. I was a bit cynical about war aims and all the rest of it, but when you're on a tank and there are thousands of Italians milling around, throwing flowers at you and cheering and offering you loaves of bread and glasses of wine, you start to think, Well, perhaps I am a liberator. It goes to your head a bit. But that was the highlight — there was a lot of hard slogging before that happened.

I'd like to ask you about after the war. Coming back.
I was very unsettled after the war. I'd had five years of my life taken away from me, but I shouldn't grizzle about that because I had marvellous experiences I wouldn't have had otherwise. I wasn't unsettled in terms of being wounded or suffering from traumas as many unfortunates were. I was in good health and I had my life ahead of me, but I was very restless. I think largely because I'd had a taste of travel, and that's an incurable disease. I'd had experiences that I felt I had to get down on paper, and I did. I wrote a manuscript which was turned down by several

publishers. About ten years later I was listening to a morning radio session and this lady was saying how lovely it was to get the children away to kindy and sit down at the typewriter and tap out another story. I got furious. I thought, She makes it all sound so nice and easy and I found it damn hard, and I still do, but I was so wild about it that I went to the drawer and I got out that manuscript and I knocked it into shape.

Gordon had originally written an autobiography, but he turned it into a novel when he rewrote it. **A Gun in My Hand** *was published by Pegasus Press in 1959.*

I wanted to call it *The Returned Man*, but the publisher said, 'No, a lot of people overseas wouldn't understand that.' That could well be a New Zealand expression. I also called it *Up the Strada* because that was a common expression we had: 'We're off up the strada.' My main memory of the war was marching along, up a strada, in a row of men, heading towards the next river.

I wanted to put down what I felt about the war, and I did that. I got it out of my system, I suppose, but I never got the travel out of my system. Italy had a big influence on me.

After the war, Gordon finished his university studies, completing an MA in history at Canterbury University College. He became a schoolteacher, teaching in Blenheim, Masterton and Auckland, and then at Christchurch Boys' High School. He also wrote many more books.

I was at an age where big impressions came in. Things you never forgot. Things that were said or things that were done. And I've got to say it, there is a beauty about war. Bofors tracers, blue, red, green, going through the sky, and the sight of Fortresses sailing through the sky, or a Spitfire — the loveliest plane that ever flew — at about twenty feet, going along the Senio — you never forget things like that.

I was there for the last seven months of the action and most of the time, except during the winter time, we were going forward, we were winning. If you saw a plane overhead, it might be a Focke-Wulf 190, but it was more likely to be a Spitfire. I didn't go through the hell that there must have been in Greece, Crete, Sidi Rezegh and these other places.

I followed the man in front, that's literally true. That's what I did. I kept the fellow in front of me in sight and kept close to him, particularly if I thought it was somebody who would survive. And there were people like that too. You felt that they might knock other people over, but they won't knock this fella. It's all superstition and fear. I know it's not rational, but that's what I thought. Some people had charmed lives. On the other hand, I had friends who arrived and were killed in the first action, so there you are. None of it makes any sense. It's a terrible lottery in the most terrible game of all.

INDEX